Got
Sun?

Got Sun?

200 Best Native Plants for Your Garden

CAROLYN HARSTAD

PHOTOGRAPHS BY CAROLYN HARSTAD

DRAWINGS BY JEAN VIETOR

INDIANA UNIVERSITY PRESS

BLOOMINGTON & INDIANAPOLIS

This book is a publication of

Indiana University Press
601 North Morton Street
Bloomington, Indiana 47404-3797 USA

iupress.indiana.edu

Telephone orders 800-842-6796
Fax orders 812-855-7931

MANUFACTURED IN THE UNITED STATES OF AMERICA

Library of Congress Cataloging-in-Publication Data

Harstad, Carolyn.
  Got sun? : 200 best native plants for your garden / Carolyn Harstad ;
photographs by Carolyn Harstad ; drawings by Jean Vietor.
      p. cm.
  Includes index.
  ISBN 978-0-253-00931-9 (pb : alk. paper) — ISBN 978-0-253-00940-1 (eb) 1.
Native plants for cultivation. 2. Native plant gardening. I. Title. II.
Title: 200 best native plants for your garden.
  SB439.H37 2013
  635.9'51—dc23

                        2012047302

1 2 3 4 5 18 17 16 15 14 13

*A good head and
a good heart are
always a formidable
combination.*

—Nelson Mandela

Dedicated with love to Peter

my husband,

my confidant,

and my best friend

Contents

If you are working on something exciting that you
really care about, you don't have to be pushed. The
vision pulls you.

—Steve Jobs

Preface

HOW CAN THIS BOOK HELP YOU BE A BETTER GARDENER?

My goal for *Got Sun?* is to show urban and suburban gardeners how easy it is to use native plants in the sunny areas of the yard. Here are descriptions of approximately 200 native plants, their hybrids, and cultivars that will grow in the suburbs—or in the city for that matter—and that love sun.

This book is organized with the same question–answer format and "Suggested Plant" listings that readers told me they appreciated in *Go Native!* The plants described are my personal favorites. Some of them may not work for you, but at least they will get you thinking. They are arranged from smallest to largest with commentary on bloom times and seasonal interest. Additional notes address zone hardiness, mature size, deer resistance, rain garden (for appropriate choices) planting requirements, and propagation.

Baptisia

Catalogs and plant lists from commercial nurseries and garden centers in and around my Twin Cities home include most of the selections presented here and many of the cultivars. If you live in a less metropolitan area and cannot locate them at your local garden center, encourage the owner to order and stock some native plants. Many native-plant nurseries ship plants. If all else fails, go online to order them.

Botanical names and common names appear side by side, not to confuse or intimidate, but to provide specifics to guarantee that what you want is what you get. In some cases, two plants can have the same common name. The botanical name identifies one specific plant and no other. These names, usually found within parentheses, are printed in italics to indicate the words are foreign, generally Latin or Greek. Each botanical name consists of two words. The *Genus* is always first and is always capitalized. *Genus* identifies closely related plants. For example, the genus name for Maple trees is *Acer* (pronounced A'-sir). The *species* epithet always begins with a small letter and identifies a specific subclass of the genus. There are over 100 species of Maple, including Red Maple, Sugar Maple, and Black Maple, so if a gardener wants a Red Maple, the nursery will provide the accurate tree when *Acer rubrum* is requested. The word *rubrum* is pronounced *rue' bruhm* and simply means red. Common and botanical names are both listed in the index.

Various species of native trees, shrubs, perennials, ferns, grasses, vines, and ground covers love the sun. Some will also do fine in shadier areas. A chapter about rain gardens addresses the latest hot gardening topic and will show you how rain gardens can benefit not only your own property but also the environment. I hope to help you gather ideas for foundation plantings, native selections along the property line, and information on the values of privacy biohedges.

This book will accomplish its purpose if it motivates you to plant some natives. Learn about their history. Google them, look at photographs, and decide which ones to bring into your life. Think about native plants that will zing in the sunny parts of your garden throughout the season. Get passionate and go native—and have fun while you're at it!

Friends have all things in common.

—*Plato*

Acknowledgments

I want to pay tribute to my Indianapolis friend, the late Bill Brink. I miss his friendship, his extensive knowledge and his incredible wisdom. He ignited my passion for native plants.

A special thank you to two good friends and wildflower enthusiasts: To Jean Vietor who did the exquisite drawings. I stand in awe of her artistic talent and will be forever grateful for her hours and hours of work. And to Bobbi Diehl, my copy editor, who tightened up my prose to make it all more readable. Thank you, Jean and Bobbi. I cherish our friendship.

Thanks to my editor, Linda Oblack, who encouraged me to write this book. Also to the staff of the Indiana University Press for their help and expertise.

Thanks to Marty Rice who encouraged me to join Wild Ones when we moved to Minnesota. She is a true believer in natives and shares my passion. I learned much while working with fellow members Roberta Moore and Mary Schommer on a Minnesota Science Museum grant. One of our goals was to encourage nurseries and garden centers to sell native plants. We whooped for joy when the 2012 Bachman Nursery Catalog came out with an entire section dedicated to natives.

Thanks to Mike Isensee and Chris Coudron, Dakota County Soil and Water Conservation District, for their concise rain garden and filtration basin instruction. Thanks also to Heritage Lutheran Church members Jane Fahning, Chris Nicolay, Brad and Tim Oachs, Barb Johnson, and Maria Reedstrom, who planted two filtration basins and weeded them. Other Heritage members volunteered to adopt a space to keep the landscaping in pristine condition. I appreciate their help. Special thanks to Pastor Karl Anderson for his work in the courtyard.

My Master Gardener friends are invaluable. Thanks to Cheryl and Dan Forrest and Dave Olson. We discuss native plants and gardening as we travel to meetings. Shari Mayer provided detailed instructions for winter seeding jugs. I enjoy working and learning with Judy Erickson and Faith Applequist. The visit to Trish Johnson's garden was a real plus. You will see Trish's gardening and landscaping expertise in some of my photographs.

Thanks also to my friend and neighbor, Mary von Eschen, for encouraging me to photograph the natives in her garden whenever the plants called.

I would be remiss if I did not acknowledge and thank Allan Armitage, Colston Burrell, William Cullina, Michael Dirr, Ken Druse, Guy Sternberg, Douglas Tallamy, and Jim Wilson. These and other researchers and garden writers provided data and insights to guide me as I wrote this book.

Thank you to Mary M. Walker, librarian of the New England Wildflower Society, who compiled an initial list of native-plant societies that I updated. She made my job of updating easier as I searched the Web. It is amazing how much information is available with a simple click of a mouse.

Whenever I experience a computer dilemma, I call my brother and he solves it. Thanks "my-Dave-genius bar!" And to Joanie: my email buddy, sister, and kindred spirit.

Grandsons Jake (seven years old) and Alex (four years old) carefully tended the Monarch caterpillars I sent for them to raise. Daughter-in-law Tiffany made sure the tiny striped Monarch babies had plenty of milkweed to chomp so they could grow to become beautiful butterflies. It was a joy to watch the boys as they experienced this adventure.

A special thank you to my five children, Linda, Karen, Mark, Kristen, and Dave, who sent emails and encouraged me with phone calls and hugs when they were nearby. An extra thanks to Karen who lives four doors up the street from us and fixed many meals so I could keep writing and to Linda for helping with the final proof reading.

Finally I want to thank Peter, my husband since 1957, who is always there for me. He read the entire manuscript repeatedly, revised and clarified my prose, gave suggestions for cutting this or adding that, and improved it with his editing skills. He is my gardening buddy and a special part of my life.

Bebb's Willow

Got
Sun?

The more natives you incorporate into your garden, the happier the little creatures in your neighborhood will be.

—Douglas W. Tallamy

1.
Got Sun?
Choose Natives for
Your Garden

As I opened my front door, I looked down at two anxious little faces. Our eight-year-old neighbor girl and her blonde friend asked, "Can we catch butterflies in your yard?" "Of course," I replied, "but you probably have some in your yard too." "Oh no," they both said solemnly, "you have the only yard with lots of butterflies."

Not long after our 2003 move from Indiana to Minnesota, I attended a Wild Ones native plant conference. A landscape design professor from the University of Michigan was the keynote speaker. She had recently done a study on how people wanted their yard to look. The majority of those surveyed replied that they aspired for it to look like their neighbors'. And that is true of most people. Unfortunately, their omnipresent turfgrass lawns are sterile, neither attracting nor keeping birds, butterflies, and other wildlife content enough to stick around. Few yards include many native plants.

Our house is a typical two-story house in a relatively new neighborhood. We are the resident grandparents in this small, close-knit community just south of Minne-

Butterfly Weed with
Monarch butterfly

apolis. When we purchased this house, the seller boasted, "My lawn is the best in the neighborhood. Bar none." And it truly was lush and beautiful. He graciously added, "I know you are a gardener so if you want to come and do any gardening before you move in, you are welcome to do so." I thanked him politely but declined while thinking silently, "If you knew what I plan to do with your beautiful 'best-in-the-neighborhood' lawn, you probably would not sell the house to me."

Homebuyers often change carpets and wallpaper, or redo the exterior house color. Eventually we also redesign outdoor living spaces to suit our individual tastes so that one owner's perfect lawn becomes another's native plant garden. Sometimes it goes the other way. When C. Colston Burrell, noted wildflower author, lived "practically in the shadow of the great skyscrapers of Minneapolis," he wrote, "Before I started gardening, I saw no butterflies here." He designed his quarter-acre yard like a native plant community "that met the needs of birds, butterflies, and other wildlife as well." I saw him after he sold that house to move back East and asked if he had revisited his old Minnesota property since his move. "Yes," Cole replied sadly. "The new owners ripped out the natives and planted turfgrass."

We did the opposite. Within days of moving in we hired a landscaping contractor to bring in his best garden soil mixture and pile it in selected areas on the existing rock-filled glacial soil in our back yard. Plants in these shady raised beds have grown and flourished. Slowly but surely we have rolled back the turfgrass. Now only a small ribbon of it leads from one side of the back yard to the other. The lush grass on the too-steep-to-mow hillside became a forgiving garden, filled with so many plants that weed seeds cannot get enough light to germinate. Our front yard has evolved from "perfect lawn" into multiple gardens filled with sun-loving natives including Purple Coneflowers, tall blue Liatris, bright orange Butterfly Weed, and even a three-stalk clump of Common Milkweed. A garden on the other side of the driveway is filled with tall prairie plants. Nearby, a horizontally branched flowering crabapple blooms and grows in the midst of another garden of shade-tolerant natives. When we replaced our severely cracked concrete driveway with pavers, neighborhood joggers, bikers, and even drivers stopped by to comment and chat. More often than not, conversation turned to my native plantings.

The best news of all is that throughout the neighborhood, homeowners are gradually digging up their turf, enlarging existing gardens, and creating new ones. My husband believes that his "native plant lady" is influencing attitudes. Folks who unwittingly sprayed weed killer on Thalictrum or Wild Geranium have learned to identify these natives. New paths wind through their wooded spaces, and neighbors delight in knowing the names of woodland wildflowers. When we came here, buckthorn dominated the wooded areas behind each home. It provided privacy, leafed out early, and lost its leaves late, but nothing else flourished under its selfish branches. Now our neighborhood association helps residents destroy this alien and encourages rejuvenation with native trees and shrubs that provide color, flowers, and fruit, and attract birds and wildlife.

I really dig native plants! Their roots run deep and their virtues abound. They are amazing. However, when I wrote *Go Native!* I was surprised to discover that my passion was far from universal. In fact, in 1999 few gardening books touted native plants as a preferred option for gardeners. Purchasing them was next to impossible. Landscapers and garden center owners turned up their noses at the idea of natives in the garden. "It will look like a weed patch," was the most common observation.

Native-plant enthusiasts in the 1990s ordered from the few mail-order websites that catered to their interests. The only other option was to rescue doomed wildflowers from construction sites. I haunted every site I learned of, and armed with boots, gloves, hat, bug spray, shovel, and the familiar plastic bags I saved from grocery shopping, I would arrive at the crack of dawn. I became such a familiar sight that heavy equipment operators would wave, grin, and yell, "At it again, Carolyn?" Then they would continue bulldozing while I scampered about digging and rescuing as many native wildflowers as my limited time allowed.

This past decade has witnessed a decided change in the way people use natives in private landscapes. Now these great plants enjoy acceptance in the world of gardeners, landscapers, urbanites, and nursery owners. Signs at local garden centers advertise each native plant and provide information about zone hardiness, mature size, and other qualities. Seminars and symposiums inform John Q. Gardener of their value. Magazines feature articles on these hardy plants. Lists of native alternatives for troublesome exotics are readily available, and many more native-plant books have come out since Indiana University Press published *Go Native!* in 1999. But what many fail to realize is that a large number of the favorite perennials they routinely plant are natives. Allan Armitage has asked, "How many of your neighbors even know that purple coneflower is a native?"

Native species are perfectly programmed to attract and nurture butter-flies, desirable insects, birds, and wildlife. That is the main reason I am so passionate about having these incredible achievers in suburban gardens. But I freely admit that some of the species are not as well behaved as many would like. In fact, some may even be classified as overachievers. Native plants were growing here when European settlers first arrived, so they easily win the title of survivor. These are the plants that do not need extra water, extra fertil-izer, or extra pampering to thrive. In some difficult sites, survival is actually accomplished by propagation. Some natives seem to increase exponentially either by running, wantonly seeding, or suckering. What is great for survival may frustrate gardeners seeking low maintenance. This may be why neatnik gardeners insist natives are weedy and refuse to even consider them.

Hybridizers are constantly working to produce gardenworthy cultivars and hybrids with more compact plant sizes, larger and more colorful flow-ers, longer bloom periods, less necessity to deadhead, intense fall leaf color, heavier fruiting, or better disease resistance. And they are trying to calm that exuberant rambunctiousness in favor of more "civilized" behavior without losing a native's ability to survive.

What is a cultivar anyway? The word simply means a "cultivated variety" with distinguishing traits. A new cultivar may come from a seedling that was open pollinated by bees, or from a seedling intentionally pollinated by a hu-man attempting to achieve some specific purpose in the resulting offspring. The International Code of Nomenclature describes a cultivar as "an assem-blage of plants that (a) has been selected for a particular character or combi-nation of characters. (b) is distinct, uniform, and stable in these characters, and (c) when propagated by appropriate means, retains those characters."

A hybrid, on the other hand, results when a "breeder selects two plants that produce identical offspring when self-pollinated and cross-pollinates them to produce a seed that combines desirable characteristics of 'traits' from both parents." However you define it, cultivars and hybrids are not identical to the species, but may possess more gardenworthy traits.

So what about using cultivars and hybrids? Purists will frown and fuss and complain, "What? Cultivars? Hybrids? I want a book about *native* plants." But remember—this is a gardening book, not a book about authentic prairie or woodland restoration. It is a book to encourage urban and suburban home-owners to incorporate native perennials into their flower gardens, choose na-tive shrubs for foundation plantings, and plant native trees.

Even though I am passionate about using the true native species as my first choice, I have never been a purist. I have always mixed natives, cultivars, and even well behaved exotics in my gardens. Why not? My ancestors were not Native Americans, but even though they are not natives most of them became responsible citizens. As the descendant of immigrants, I do not believe all non-natives are bad. I just make sure I recognize and avoid any exotic species that become invasive thugs in the environment.

I unabashedly include many interesting cultivars in my repertoire. I agree with Allan Armitage's premise: in *Armitage's Native Plants for North American Gardens,* he asserts that if gardeners who refuse to plant native species would begin with a few native cultivars they might overcome their initial resistance. "Cultivars are the gardeners' candy store," he continues. "If you like purple coneflower, a dozen choices now await you." He questions, "Should cultivars be called native? I don't know—should rap be called music? It is simply a matter of opinion." Armitage believes that "garden-improved cultivars, both selections and hybrids, will only help mainstream gardeners further embrace the world of native plants." With cultivars continually being added to the commercial inventory, the choices in the candy store have become irresistible. Just remember to include some of the "meat and potatoes" species in your gardens too.

What you choose to plant in your landscape makes a difference. A few years ago, an article in *Wildflower* detailed the disappearance of Celandine Poppy (*Stylophorum diphyllum*) in parts of Canada due to habitat disturbance. This plant germinates easily and seeds readily, as any midwestern gardener can attest. Celandine or Wood Poppy puts on a spectacular spring floral display and then blooms on and off all summer long, repeatedly surprising observers with yet another glistening golden gem. Incorporating it into private landscapes in areas where it is at risk provides insurance against extirpation.

Habitat destruction is the primary cause for the decline of the striking Royal Catchfly (*Silene regia*) in the wild. Now considered a threatened species in the Midwest, it too can successfully germinate and grow in conventional perennial borders. Hummingbirds frolic above these tall, bright red flowers. Mass plantings bring universal admiration. Give Royal Catchfly the sunny location it needs, and it will multiply. And just imagine how thrilled your hummers will be!

We know how important the South American rainforest is for future medical discoveries. The same may be true of North American native plants.

Echinacea, an herbal remedy derived from Purple Coneflower, is sold to boost the immune system. Yew (*Taxus canadensis*) provides Taxol, one of the most powerful drugs available for treating cancer. Pawpaw (*Asimina triloba*) and Mayapple (*Podophyllum peltatum*) are two other natives with promising cancer-fighting abilities.

But how much difference can one person make? Consider the survival of the Franklin tree. It was doomed to extinction when John Bartram collected seeds in 1765 from the few remaining trees along the banks of the Altamaha River in Georgia. He propagated and planted them in 1728 near Philadelphia in the first botanical garden in America. Bartram named this beautiful tree in honor of his friend and fellow Philadelphian, Benjamin Franklin, and now gardeners can purchase Franklin trees for their suburban landscapes.

A century ago, powerful industrialists coveted the Indiana Dunes on the shore of Lake Michigan as their rightful place to expand. A few individuals who recognized the stark beauty and the unusual flora and fauna of the area fought to preserve it, and eventually prevailed. There are times when concerned citizens need to explain that a particular development plan might endanger a rare species.

Why do I feel so passionate about using native plants? Several years ago during a break at a native-plant conference, I visited with the featured speaker, native-plant author and photographer Andy Wasowski. He and I commiserated about the all-too-prevalent "anywhere USA" and agreed that regardless of where one travels, most urban areas look the same "from sea to shining sea." The only place where the change in environment is readily apparent is in the undeveloped spaces between cities and towns. When we choose plants that are native to our area, we create a sense of place. In addition, we help to restore lost ecosystems that human development has destroyed.

Milkweed is the only larval food source Monarch caterpillars will eat, but these plants are becoming ever more scarce in our environment. You may not want to incorporate Common Milkweed (*Asclepias syriaca*) into your perennial border as I have, but what about adding soft pink Swamp or Marsh Milkweed (*A. incarnata*) or bright orange Butterfly Weed (*A. tuberosa*)? Monarch larvae will feed on these too. Our vanishing milkweed plants need help and so do our Monarchs. Gardeners can make a difference.

Are there butterflies in my yard? Absolutely. All summer I observe Monarchs flocking to my milkweed plants and my grandchildren hunt for their caterpillars. Beautiful Black and Tiger Swallowtails gather nectar; Painted

Ladies, Mourning Cloaks, Buckeye butterflies, and many that I do not recognize enjoy life here. I watch the antics of goldfinches, cardinals, robins, Black-capped Chickadees, nuthatches, and even a pair of Pileated Woodpeckers. Hummingbirds and Sphinx Moths zing about like tiny helicopters. The small, wooded conservation area behind the house is filled with native wildflowers instead of the resident buckthorn that plagued this entire neighborhood a decade ago. Deer wander through, rabbits hop about, a red fox occasionally ambles along the mulch path that snakes through the woods, squirrels tear up and down the trees hopping from branch to branch, an owl hoots in the night, and songbirds constantly flit about, singing, nesting, and raising their young in full sight of our deck.

Native plants are incredible wildlife magnets. As Cole Burrell wisely said, "Through proper design and planting, we can give a home to creatures that are often shut out of our cities and suburbs." Plant even a few natives and "they" will come. Guaranteed! I hope that by the time you read the last page of this book, you too will feel passionate about gardening with natives.

Bee Balm

2.

Planting
Requirements

What Is Necessary
for Success?

The mostly unrecognized truth is that our yards and gardens need to function in much the same way as a wilderness area does.

—Marlene Condon

This book is full of specific details about hundreds of native plants. Yet several general considerations pertain to all of them. Success is determined by choosing a site for each plant with proper light, moisture, soil type, and pH. Each plant description includes a segment entitled Plant Requirements. Most are brief and not overly complex. You may wonder, "What is average, well-drained garden soil?" so let's begin with soil.

Soil

Soil is usually sand, silt, clay, or a combination, often referred to as loam. *Sandy* soil has the largest particles. It is impossible to make a ball out of moistened sandy soil that will hold its shape. Water drains quickly so this type of soil often loses nutrients. Moisture-loving plants need additional water in sandy sites.

Clay has the smallest particles so although it hangs onto nutrients and retains water, it has poor drainage. Plants that enjoy wet or consistently moist sites often thrive in clay soil, but those that require well-drained soil do not. Their roots will rot. All plants

Wild Petunia

need a certain amount of air around their roots. Clay is considered heavy soil and can dry rock hard in drought. Make a ball out of clay soil and it will remain a ball. Some potters make permanent figures or containers with clay soil. I have a small statue of a woman that my son purchased in Haiti. It is as hard as if it had been fired, but was dried naturally in the hot sun.

Silt particles are medium sized. Its texture feels less gritty than sand, but not as smooth as clay soil. Silt is considered rich soil, is generally well drained, but can become too dry in the heat of the day. When it is dry it resembles dark sand.

Loamy soil is a combination of all three and is the best choice for most plants because it contains the required nutrients, is loose and easy to dig or plant in, allows roots to delve deeply, retains just enough moisture, yet drains well. It will make a loose ball that crumbles easily between your fingers.

And what is "average, well-drained garden soil?" Many term it "ordinary" garden soil. It is neither too acidic nor too alkaline. Ideally it is as close to loam as possible, but we do not all have loamy soil on our property. Work with whatever is present. If necessary, add just enough organic material to retain decent moisture or enough sand to drain properly. The soil in my yard is primarily clay. So do I amend it? No more than necessary. But I do occasionally add a little compost. And as I mentioned earlier, when we first moved here we purchased a mixture of "garden loam" from a landscaper to put on top of the rock-hard glacial soil that was left after the house construction. I try to choose plants that will thrive in existing soil without major amendments but builders often leave gardeners no choice. If your soil is really terrible, then tweak it until it seems just right.

Whatever your soil situation, remember that sunny prairie natives do best on soil that is not overly rich. With too many nutrients they will grow too tall and flop, so give them tough love and encourage deep root growth.

Why is pH important?

What does pH mean? According to the *American Heritage Science Dictionary,* "the letters pH stand for potential of hydrogen." Hmmm. That definition does not help this scientifically challenged gardener. I delved deeper and learned that, simply stated, pH is a measure of acidity or alkalinity between 0 and 14. Did you know that distilled water is 7, rainwater is 6.5, human blood is 7.4, and lemonade is 3.5?

What about soil? Soil with a pH of 7 is neutral; below 7 is considered acidic; over 7 is alkaline. Most garden soils are between 4 and 8. Most common garden plants do best in slightly acidic soil with a pH between 5.5 and 6.5. Correct pH is crucial. Necessary nutrients bond to the soil particles and will not release to the plant when the pH is wrong. Acid-loving plants in alkaline clay soil cannot absorb necessary nutrients and become chlorotic. One year I noticed that my Red Maple developed unusual bright green veins in chartreuse leaves. I recognized it as an iron deficiency, added a soil acidifier, and now my tree has normal deep green leaves. Left untreated the tree would have died from the top down. We have all noticed yellow leaves on Pin Oaks planted in cities with an abundance of clay soil. The pH is wrong for the species. So even if we do not fully understand the chemistry, we know that it is important to test the soil to determine what additives, if any, are necessary to adjust the pH so that the plants you choose can effectively absorb the proper nutrients. Otherwise they will weaken, become diseased, and die. In some cases, the best solution is to back off and look for plants that can handle the prevailing pH extreme.

What about moisture?

We can reduce maintenance by combining plants with similar needs. A wet site is just that—wet or marshy. Except for a pond or a natural marsh at the edge of a property, few home landscapes include this type of environment. Even the bottom of a rain garden is not wet all the time. Moist, or "continually moist," is the more common requirement for home gardens. Moisture-lovers do not like drought and some will not tolerate any dryness. To avoid continual watering, add compost to the site and mulch heavily to reduce evaporation and keep the soil cool and moist. Or choose plants with less demanding moisture requirements.

Many of the plants in this book are considered prairie plants. These prefer drier planting sites, yet even a drought-tolerant plant needs occasional deep watering to survive. Most plants thrive with an inch of water per week. Set a small plastic rain gauge in each garden to measure. A good rainstorm is the ideal way to water, but the heavens do not always open on cue, so occasional supplemental watering may be necessary. Keep all new plantings well watered until they are established. For newly planted trees and shrubs, instead of using overhead sprinklers or even a garden hose, pick a day of the week and give each a weekly 5-gallon bucketful of water during the growing season until late in the fall.

Light in the garden

Full Sun: Plants requiring full sun need a minimum of six hours of direct sunlight each day. Those hours may come in an unbroken six-hour chunk, or intermittently. In some locations, plants will get full sun nearly all day.

Part Sun/Part Shade: Some of my plant descriptions list one term, some the other. These are basically interchangeable, meaning at least 3–6 hours of sunlight every day. The hottest sun is always the afternoon sun. Plants listed as part sun appreciate more time in the sun and can usually tolerate some afternoon sun. Plants identified as part shade may suffer in the afternoon heat especially in midsummer so may do better with a little longer protection from the sun.

Shade: Plants receiving less than three hours of light, either direct or filtered, need to be shade tolerant. Most shade tolerant plants are found in woodlands, although many will grow in some degree of shade, as I learned when researching *Got Shade?* (2003).

Is it possible to propagate native plants?

Dakota County Master Gardeners encourage gardeners to try winter seeding. Poke four holes for drainage in the bottom of a clean, uncovered, translucent gallon milk jug. With a sharp knife, cut the jug horizontally from one side of the handle across the front of the jug to the other side of the handle. Do not remove the handle. This creates a hinged opening. Put two inches of inexpensive soil in the bottom of the jug, water thoroughly, and when drained, press seeds generously into the damp soil. Water lightly. Use a separate milk jug for each type of seed. With a permanent marker, write the name of each type of seed on a popsicle stick or plastic marker and put it inside the jug. Close jug and tape shut with clear duct tape. Identify the seed on the outside of each jug. Move the milk jugs outside for the winter and leave them until spring. They can be on any side of the house except the south side. Condensation forming inside the jug indicates no additional water is necessary. If condensation ceases, water lightly. In spring, when temperatures warm, remove the tape and crack the jug slightly open. Transplant seedlings into pots in spring to continue to grow until the ground warms.

I have done my share of dividing existing plants, transplanting seedlings, and growing plants from seed, but I am certainly no plant propagation expert. Therefore, for propagation recommendations for each described plant, I relied on such authorities as William Cullina, Executive Director of the Coastal Maine Botanical Gardens in Boothbay, Maine. Formerly the nursery manager and chief propagator for the New England Wild Flower Society, Bill knows whereof he speaks. Another trustworthy expert is Michael Dirr, professor of horticulture at the University of Georgia. His books are invaluable.

Can I plant seeds from cultivars or hybrids?

Cultivars are identified with single quotes. A hybrid is identified with a multiplication symbol × between two names indicating the resulting plant is a cross between those two species. Hybrids cannot be duplicated by planting their seed, nor can you predict what you will get when you plant that seed. If you want the real thing you must purchase a hybridized plant. It is illegal to propagate many of the newer cultivars, but do not despair. Most hybrids and cultivars are readily available at the local garden center or online.

As you pick and choose trees remember the word *provenance*. Provenance means that a particular plant was grown from seeds gathered in a particular area; therefore it is genetically adapted to that region and will perform more dependably than similar plants grown from seeds from far away. For trees and other plants too, this is an important concept to note.

As you search, be aware that plants grow, even while you are not paying attention or are on vacation, so find out how tall and wide each plant will become. Knowing the mature size of a plant can save you a ton of heartache and headaches. Checking the mature size of a plant is tantamount to the old adage, "work smarter, not harder." You want to plant something and let it grow, not try to figure out where you will have to replant it or how it will need to be trimmed. Or worse yet, destroy it because it overgrew the space and is simply too big.

Planting

Bare root trees or shrubs, stored in cold storage warehouses, remain dormant until specialty nurseries offer them for sale in early spring. Following purchase, it is imperative to keep the roots moist and plant as soon as possible. Dig a hole deep and wide enough to hold the roots without crowding. Put a small mound of dirt in the center of the hole, set the tree on the mound, and spread the roots to the bottom of the planting space. At this point, Willard

Heiss, an Indiana friend, always dropped in what he called tree candy, a slow-release fertilizer tablet. Use enough soil to hold the tree in place and fill the planting hole with water. Once the hole has drained, fill in the remaining soil, tamping the ground firmly to eliminate air pockets and keep the tree upright. Stake if necessary. Bare root plants are easy to transport and transplant but are only available in early spring.

During the growing season, trees are offered in a variety of planting sizes and are available as small potted specimens or as large balled-and-burlapped trees. Either can be planted anytime during the growing season but spring or early fall are preferred. Dig a hole no deeper than the bottom of the pot or the ball, but about 6 inches wider. Roughen the soil on the sides and in the bottom of the hole, move the tree into the hole, slice and pull down the burlap, and then fill the hole with water. Once it has totally drained, add the rest of the soil. Plant the tree at the same level it is planted in the pot, making sure the flare of the trunk is visible about an inch above the top of the soil and not covered with either soil or mulch. Planting a tree too deep is one of the most common causes of early tree death.

Pruning

Shaping by proper pruning is especially important when a tree is young. Remove crossed branches or extremely narrow crotches. Prune each branch just above the collar, not flush with the trunk, so the wound heals quickly. The collar is the slightly thickened area where the base of the branch attaches to the trunk.

Occasionally a door-to-door tree pruner will offer to "top" your trees. Tell him no thanks and send him on his way. We have all observed those sad tree-amputees, especially near or under overhead wires. The hefty stubs seldom heal properly and provide easy access for disease and insect damage through the open wounds. Moreover, water shoots sprout around the outer edges of the wounds and do nothing for the appearance of the formerly beautiful tree. Always insist that any large branches are pruned back to the collar, not just "whacked off at the elbow." Your tree will thank you.

Pruning paint is neither necessary nor recommended. Painting the wounds can seal in moisture, encourage disease, and delay necessary tissue formation.

3.
Planning a Garden?

Start with Trees

Trees . . . frame, anchor, and connect all the elements to the sky.

—Ezra Haggard

Trees, regardless of size, come in a variety of shapes, including spreading, rounded, open, pyramidal, or weeping. Trees of any size or shape can provide cool shade, beautiful fall color, bark interest, and even spring flowers. They give shelter to birds, offer larval food and nectar for butterflies, and encourage wildlife to check out your property. Walk through your neighborhood or watch as you drive through suburban areas to determine what sizes and shapes command your attention and might contribute to your overall landscape design.

Is your property brand new with a newly built house and a blank yard just waiting for help? Or does it already have mature trees casting long shadows or creating dancing patterns of light and shade throughout the day? The title of this book is *Got Sun?* It assumes you *do* have sun and that you yearn to learn what to plant in those sunny spots.

Talking about shade need not distract us here, but gardeners must deal with realities. Houses cast shadows. Let us also assume that even if big trees are not already growing on your property, at least one is on your wish list. No, you don't need a huge tree, but

Tulip Poplar

you are probably like the sentimental Tin Man, who, when the Wizard of Oz tells him, "You don't *need* a heart," responds earnestly, "But I still *want* one."

Large shade trees are crucial landscaping components, contributing much wherever they grow, and because these forest giants take longer to mature than small specimens, for those of us who "still want one," these big boys must get our attention before we discuss the little guys.

So, for just a moment, let us discuss large trees. Here are some of my favorite forest giants, all of whom love the sun. Note their mature height. Few small properties can accommodate more than one or two, so exercise restraint. It is unwise to overplant anything, especially large trees. Many grow slowly and may not reach maximum height in your lifetime, but you should know how big a plant might get before you grab your spade. As Susan Roth says, "Planting the wrong tree in the wrong place can be an expensive mistake."

Suggested Large Trees

(Plant these where their shadows will not interfere with sites for sun gardens)

Black Gum (*Nyssa sylvatica*)

Zones 4–9
30–50 feet

Black Gum is also called Black Tupelo or Sour Gum. It grows at a slow to medium rate with a mature spread of 20–30 feet. Birds relish the dark fruit that ripens in the fall. This plant is dioecious, so for best fruit production you need to plant both a male and female, or make sure a mate is in the neighborhood. The bark on fully mature trees is often described as "alligator hide." Black Gum is a Missouri Botanical Plant of Merit winner, which comes as no surprise. Homeowners will delight in the dependable striking autumn leaf show. Black Gum is a larval food host of the Hebrew moth.

The new leaf growth of the cultivar 'Wildfire' is red in spring, becomes shiny green in summer, and then explodes into an unimaginable fiery red autumn display. 'Autumn Cascades' is a weeping form.

PLANTING REQUIREMENTS

Plant in moist, well-drained, slightly acidic soil in full sun. This adaptable tree will tolerate drought and flooding. Provenance is important. To be assured of the most intense leaf color, choose a specific tree at the nursery in the fall.

PROPAGATION

Can be grown from seed, but care should be taken to cold-stratify the seeds, especially in warm areas. This tree has a deep taproot, and transplanting can be a challenge. Best results may be obtained by planting a potted specimen.

Red Maple (*Acer rubrum*)
Zones 3–9

40–70 feet

Whenever someone asks for "the best fast-growing tree for my landscape" I recommend a Red Maple. It has the same fast-growing qualities as Silver Maple, but few of the drawbacks. Its branches are not as susceptible to ice storm damage. It has pretty, pinkish-red hanging flowers that cover the tree in spring, creating a rosy glow in the landscape. The leaves, usually light green with whitish backs and red leaf stems, cover this nicely shaped tree in summer, then change to brilliant shades of red in the fall.

Popular cultivars with dependable fall foliage include 'Red Sunset', 'Autumn Flame', 'October Glory', and 'Northwood'. The new columnar cultivar 'Red Rocket' may be a good choice for a small yard. 'Red Supersonic' is another narrow cultivar growing 40 feet tall but only about 10 feet wide. 'Brandywine' has red-purple fall color and matures at 25 feet, but is only 12 feet wide. 'Sun Valley' gets 35 feet tall and is a good street tree.

PLANTING REQUIREMENTS

Red Maple will tolerate just about any type of soil as long as it is either neutral or slightly acidic. It dislikes soil that is too alkaline, prefers consistent moisture, and does not fare well in drought.

PROPAGATION

Red Maple seeds germinate easily. This fast-growing tree can change from a small whip to a good-sized tree in about a dozen years. It is usually easy to find at the garden center in a variety of sizes. About fifteen years ago I planted a whip and although the bright yellow fall foliage was striking, I was disappointed my Red Maple did not have red leaves. Visit a nursery in fall after the leaves have turned to find the color you want.

River Birch (*Betula nigra*)
Zones 4–9

40–70 feet

Deer resistant

The rosy cinnamon exfoliating bark on River Birch is its dominant feature. It has delicate yellow leaves in the fall. River Birch becomes very large with age, so this is not a tree for the center of a small flower garden. (Small, tidy cultivars are described in the "Small Trees" section later in this chapter). If you are determined to include a full-sized River Birch in a garden space, site it near the corner of your house and dig a curving garden out from its trunk into the yard. This may be a good idea because turfgrass often languishes beneath this multi-trunked tree, especially when it is mature. If garden plants do not thrive, choose a hardy ground cover.

'Heritage', a 1990 award winning cultivar with white peeling bark, is reminiscent of Paper Birch, but without the danger of premature death from the Bronze Birch Borer. It grows 40–45 feet tall. Heat-tolerant 'Dura Heat' is another desirable full sized cultivar.

PLANTING REQUIREMENTS

Prefers moist, well-drained soils, but once established will tolerate just about any site. As its name suggests, River Birch flourishes near streams and can withstand occasional flooding.

PROPAGATION

Plant seeds in the fall for spring germination or root softwood cuttings. This species is easy to transplant and is readily available in the nursery trade.

Oak (*Quercus* spp.)

Zones 3–8

50–70 feet

Oaks are slow-growing, magnificent landscape trees with striking fall color. When we visited the National September 11 Memorial and Museum site in New York City in November 2011, I realized the newly planted oak trees exactly followed the perimeter of the unusual waterfall reflecting pools and would contribute to the winter landscape with their persistent leaves. Even though oaks are deciduous, these trees "never give up," steadfastly holding onto their autumn leaves until new spring growth appears and life begins anew. This trait seems to fit the 9/11 site. Named *Reflecting Absence* by architect Michael Arad, the pools are an exact footprint of the former Twin Towers and effectively reflect their absence. Four hundred twenty-five Swamp White Oaks, selected by landscape architect Peter Walker, provide an effective sound barrier, muffling the clanging noise of the city even as they maintain a peaceful calm within the memorial. These magnificent trees symbolize hope, renewal, and strength. Several oak species in our woods delight me when their new leaves suddenly emerge in spring.

There are hundreds of oak species so do a little research and choose one that is appropriate for your area and planting site. The beautiful Red Oak (*Q. rubra*) is probably most at risk for Oak Wilt, spread by an insect called *Ceratocystis fagacearum*. If you must prune an oak, do so between November 1 and March 1 when the tree is dormant. White Oak (*Q. alba*), 80–100 feet tall, is not as susceptible to Oak Wilt as Red Oak.

PLANTING REQUIREMENTS

Most oaks prefer neutral to acidic, moist, well-drained soil in full sun. Red Oak can tolerate more shade than most. Pin Oak (*Q. palustris*), 60–70 feet tall, demands moist, acidic soil. Chinkapin Oak (*Q. muehlenbergii*), 40–50 feet tall, is not as fussy.

PROPAGATION

Collect acorns in the fall and lay them on their sides to germinate in spring. Squirrels and other rodents also collect acorns to store for winter, so protect your planting site. Most oak species are readily available from nursery growers. Spring planting is recommended.

Sugar Maple (*Acer saccharum*)
Zones 3–8
60–75 feet
Sun/Part Sun

Native Sugar Maples have a lovely shape, grow slowly but dependably, and are one of the prettiest large native trees available. If you love fresh maple syrup, here is your chance to make your own. And if you yearn for a large tree with fantastic fall color, choose a Sugar Maple.

Better yet, pick 'Fall Fiesta' for incredible leaf shades of bright yellow, brilliant orange, and deep red. 'Flax Mill' maintains an oval shape and is resistant to sun scald, while 'Sugar Cone' is a pyramidal dwarf cultivar with a very dense crown. It seldom exceeds 20 feet so it may be a good choice for the smaller landscape.

PLANTING REQUIREMENTS
Native Sugar Maples need moist, well-drained soil. They suffer in drought, so hybridizers have worked diligently to develop more drought-tolerant cultivars. 'Green Mountain' and 'Legacy' are good examples of these recent introductions.

PROPAGATION
Plant ripe seeds in the fall. Sugar Maples can be found in nearly any nursery that sells shade trees.

Tulip Tree (*Liriodendron tulipifera*)
Zones 4–9
70–100 feet (and up!)
A favorite of Thomas Jefferson at Monticello, the Tulip Tree (aka Tulip Poplar) is a tall, straight, fast-growing tree. It is the state tree of Indiana, Kentucky, and Tennessee. The unique leaves have a tulip shape and become golden yellow in the fall. After the tree is several years old, pale yellow and bright orange tulip-like flowers appear, opening in late spring. Locate a Tulip Tree away from driveways and sidewalks because aphids love the flowers and will drop their sticky dew on whatever is below. It is necessary to rake fallen petals—a downside for neatniks. But that is a small price to pay for the early season beauty.

Northern gardeners may find this tree difficult to establish, although there is a magnificent specimen growing at the Minnesota Landscape Arboretum. I stood at the base and looked up . . . and up and up the tallest, straightest trunk imaginable. Tiger Swallowtails seek out the Tulip Tree for their larval needs and hummingbirds enjoy the nectar of the showy flowers.

'Compactum' and 'Ardis' are smaller, more compact cultivars of the species and more suitable choices for the smaller suburban property. 'Compactum' is globe-shaped. Striking leaf variegation has been bred into 'Mediopictum' and 'Aureopictum'. 'Fastigiatum,' a narrow, columnar tree, is difficult to find in the trade. The compact upright cultivar 'Emerald City', hardy to Zone

6, only reaches 50 feet tall and 25 feet wide at maturity. It has darker green leaves and brighter yellow fall color than the species.

PLANTING REQUIREMENTS
Plant in an open space in moist, well-drained soil in full sun. Maintain adequate moisture during the growing season, especially if the summer becomes hot and dry.

PROPAGATION
Plant ripe seeds in the fall, root cuttings, or purchase trees from your local nursery in the spring.

Time to get back to gardening in the sun

Now that we have ideas for a substantial shade tree or two, let us talk about small- or medium-sized native trees you might add without unduly compromising that all-important component—sunlight.

Here are some small trees that will mature at less than 12 feet that you might incorporate into your garden, or at least plant on its border. Most are cultivars of the species bred for their tiny size. Gardeners can safely add vertical interest to small sunny spaces with these mini-specimens. There is no danger they will crowd the area to distraction. Nor will they cast an inor- dinate amount of shade on the sun-lovers beneath their small branches.

Suggested Very Small Trees, Less Than 12 Feet

Tiger Eye Sumac (*Rhus typhina* 'Bailtiger')
Zones 4–8
3–6 feet
Deer and rabbit resistant

Tiger Eye Sumac is an example of "sporting." Discovered in a nursery planting of *R. typhina* 'Laciniata' in 1985, this unique small tree has show-stopping color, changing from chartreuse in spring to bright yellow in summer and to yellow, red, and orange in the fall. Japanese Maple lovers in colder climates may find this little tree with its long, thin, finely dissected leaves the answer to their prayers.

The only drawback to this handsome dwarf tree is its insistence on "running." Like most native sumacs, it suckers, sending out runners in many directions, eventually creating a good-sized colony. However, it is not as aggressive as larger sumacs and the runners are not difficult to pull when they are young. Just be aware that it requires maintenance to remain a single focal point.

'Laciniata', also known as *R. typhina* 'Dissecta', is taller than Tiger Eye, growing 10–15 feet. The deeply dissected fernlike leaves can be 2 feet long and go through a cycle of change from deep green to orange, red, and yellow. It produces the familiar 8-inch-long reddish-brown "staghorn" seed clusters. This cultivar suckers heavily.

PLANTING REQUIREMENTS
Average, well-drained soil. Drought tolerant.

PROPAGATION
Transplanted suckers often die, which can be frustrating. It is reasonably priced, so just purchase a potted specimen.

'Autumn Magic' Black Chokeberry tree form (*Aronia melanocarpa*)
Zones 3–7
5–6 feet
This Bailey Nurseries 2012 introduction is a small-sized columnar tree form of the popular, dependable native shrub. Fragrant, five-petaled white flowers cover the shiny green leaves in late spring. In summer, this little beauty is laden with edible, nearly black berries, fat and juicy to tempt gardeners (if they can beat the birds to the prize). In the fall, shiny green leaves change to shades of red and purple.

PLANTING REQUIREMENTS
Average, well-drained soil in full sun. Drought tolerant once established.

PROPAGATION
This is a hybrid. Purchase potted plants at the nursery.

Dwarf River Birch (*Betula nigra* cultivars)
Zones 3–9

6–10 feet

Deer resistant

River Birch, a favorite landscaping tree described earlier in this chapter, is too massive to be incorporated into a typical perennial garden. However, several new and exciting slow-growing cultivars can easily blend into a small space, adding vertical interest.

'Little King' (aka Fox Valley®) seldom grows taller than ten feet. It has a dense, compact growth habit. The exfoliating bark exhibits shades of melon and cinnamon. In the autumn, its glowing yellow leaves provide a bright spot in the landscape.

'Summer Cascade' is a weeping form that grows 6–8 feet tall. This graceful little tree is resistant to Bronze Birch Borer and can be pruned to a single trunk. Its small, bright green leaves turn yellow in fall. In some website pictures it looks like a willowy weeper reminiscent of a slim ballerina. In other pictures it looks as if the ballerina suddenly sank to the floor with her skirt ballooning like a mushroom. In any case, this is a delightful little tree that will provide a unique look to your garden.

'Shiloh Splash' is a variegated cultivar with white-edged leaves. Some sources report the mature height at 8–12 feet at 10 years. Others list it at 20–30 feet, so to play it safe, you may want to plant this interesting birch at the edge of the garden.

PLANTING REQUIREMENTS

These dwarf birch trees all enjoy moist, well-drained soil in full sun to partial shade. All have the exfoliating bark typical of full-sized *Betula nigra* species.

Redwing 'J. N. Select' Cranberry Bush (*Viburnum trilobum*)
Zones 2–7

8–12 feet

Another Bailey Nurseries introduction for 2012 is this newly developed tree form of the native High Bush Cranberry. New leaves emerge with a red tinge and then in the fall the leaves change from green to brilliant shades of red. This plant, with its pretty white lacecap flowers and bright golden berries changing to a vibrant red, is guaranteed to be a magnet for birds and butterflies.

The shrub form, selected at Johnson's Nursery in 1983, is lovely too. It matures at 8–10 feet and makes a great hedge or specimen shrub. The plant introduction program Chicagoland Grows reports that Dr. Edward R. Hasselkus of the University of Wisconsin, Madison verified this plant as "a true *V. trilobum,* not a hybrid—unlike many other cultivars in the trade."

PLANTING REQUIREMENTS
Moist, well-drained soil in full sun. Provide extra water during periods of drought.

PROPAGATION
Purchase the tree form at the nursery.

Eastern Wahoo *(Euonymus atropurpureus)*
Zones 3–8
6–12 feet

Eastern Wahoo is often grown as a shrub. It grows taller in warmer zones, occasionally reaching as high as 20 feet. But this versatile plant can easily be pruned into a small tree by removing the lower branches. Rosy pink capsules split open in the fall and shiny, bright red-orange seeds attract birds throughout the winter. It is one of those "Wow, what is that?" plants. It may be difficult to locate in the nursery trade, but just be a squeaky wheel and squeak until you find it! Or search online.

PLANTING REQUIREMENTS
Requires consistent moisture in deep, rich, well-drained soil. Will not tolerate poor drainage.

PROPAGATION
Seeds do not germinate readily. Dirr reports that two months of cold followed by three months of warmth resulted in only 40 percent germination. Try planting cleaned, ripened seeds immediately or try to root softwood cuttings.

Leatherwood *(Dirca palustris)*
Zones 3–8
3–6 feet
Part sun/shade

Leatherwood is another small native often called a shrub. However, it nearly always grows either as a miniature tree with a single trunk, or as a clump. Adequate sunlight encourages dense growth and makes this a perfect choice to tuck into the back of a native garden.

William Cullina aptly describes the narrow, yellow flowers as "little chartreuse earrings." These delicate flowers bloom in spring. The glossy medium green leaves turn clear yellow in the fall. Golden-hued bark is handsome in the landscape through the seasons. Pliable stems can bend in nearly any direction, which explains the common name.

You may have to hunt for this little gem, but it is worth the search. Mail-order nurseries will ship.

PLANTING REQUIREMENTS

Grows best in fertile, moist soil in either full sun or partial shade. The branches have narrow crotches that may be susceptible to splitting in winters with ice or heavy snow loads. Prune young specimens to a central trunk, removing as many of the narrow crotches as possible to encourage stronger limbs.

How about medium-sized trees?

Here are some medium-sized trees that mature up to 20 feet. These are probably too large to be incorporated within the planting space but might anchor the end of a garden. I often create a kidney-shaped garden flowing out from the base of a medium-sized tree. The plants within this design get plenty of sunlight, yet the tree at the border draws attention to the entire garden and creates a handsome focal point.

As you read *Got Sun?*, you will note that some plants are listed as sun/part sun or even sun/part shade. These particular plants prefer sun but appreciate an occasional respite, especially in the heat of summer at midday. So some of the trees described below will provide that respite, yet not create a shady dilemma for the sunny gardener.

Suggested Medium-sized Trees to 20 Feet

Blackhaw Viburnum (*Viburnum prunifolium*)
Nannyberry (*Viburnum lentago*)
Zones 3–9
8–15 feet
Sun/part sun
Either of these two adaptable viburnums can be trained into handsome small trees. Nannyberry is slightly larger than Blackhaw, occasionally reaching heights of 20–25 feet. Blackhaw matures at about 12 feet. Like most viburnums, Nannyberry will tolerate some shade. Blackhaw, on the other hand, needs full sun to perform at its best. Both have large, flat, showy white flower clusters in late spring, followed by tasty, deep black berries relished by birds, wildlife, and people. Both have vibrant fall leaves in shades of deep burgundy.

PLANTING REQUIREMENTS
Provide good air circulation for Nannyberry. It is susceptible to mildew in crowded locations, but performs well in open spaces. Blackhaw and Nannyberry can tolerate either wet or dry conditions as long as the soil is well drained. Blackhaw is the more drought-tolerant of the two.

PROPAGATION
Containerized tree specimens are readily available at most nurseries.

Gray Dogwood (*Cornus racemosa*)
Zones 4–8
8–15 feet
Sun/part shade
Gray Dogwood has always been one of my favorite small native trees. It can also be grown as a multi-stemmed shrub. Delicate lacy white flowers cover the tree in spring, followed by bright white berries that hang from red stalks (pedicels). The leaves turn a deep plum-purple to burgundy-red in the fall.

Gray Dogwood is a larval food host for the Spring Azure butterfly. Birds, especially cardinals, woodpeckers, and bluebirds, enjoy the white fruits that never persist very long when these feathered friends are in the neighborhood.

'Jade' is a taller tree, often reaching 15 feet. Growing it as a clump tree similar to River Birch is recommended for best results.

PLANTING REQUIREMENTS

This little tree/shrub enjoys moist soil, but can survive drought. Its only drawback is that it suckers and can eventually form thickets if regular pruning maintenance is not performed. Locate it at the edge of your yard where it is free to roam rather than in a small formal flower garden, or resolve to pull or cut suckers as soon as they sprout.

PROPAGATION

Seeds or cuttings. Provenance is important for reliable survival.

'Princess Kay' Canada Plum (*Prunus nigra* 'Princess Kay')

Zones 3–7

10–15 feet

'Princess Kay', the well-behaved small selection of Canada Plum, was found growing in the wild in northern Minnesota near Grand Rapids. Introduced in 1986 by the Minnesota Landscape Arboretum, it makes a stunning statement in any front yard where it becomes about 10 feet wide. According to Northscaping.com, if you yearn for a tree that resembles the Japanese Cherry trees ringing the Tidal Basin in Washington, DC, look no further. White double flowers cover this lovely little tree in spring. Red fruits hang from branches covered with glossy green leaves and in the fall the tree becomes golden orange-yellow. The handsome bark is dark colored—nearly black.

The taller native Canada Plum (*P. nigra*) grows in the wild, especially in more northerly ranges. It can reach 15–20 feet at maturity.

PLANTING REQUIREMENTS

Site in loamy, well-drained soil in full sun.

PROPAGATION

Purchase at a nursery.

American Plum (*Prunus americana*)

Zones 3–8

10–18 feet

Sun/part sun

I planted several specimens of this small tree at the edge of my yard. If it has ample sunlight, the early spring clusters of highly fragrant white flowers will mature into small, edible, red plums with tasty yellow flesh, relished by wildlife (and people too!). Birds eat the ripened fruit after it falls to the ground. Autumn leaves become vibrant shades of yellow and orange. The bark is dark reddish brown. As the tree matures, it develops thorns, so I am careful to plant my trees away from the path.

PLANTING REQUIREMENTS

Drought tolerant, it thrives in average, well-drained soil. It suckers readily, so be prepared to prune regularly if you do not want a thicket. At least two of these trees are necessary to produce fruit. Plant in full sun for best flower and fruit production as well as intense fall leaf color.

PROPAGATION

Plant the seeds in the fall, or stratify them in a cold environment to be planted in spring. Softwood cuttings of young branches will root and can be planted as whips once adequate roots are established.

Fringetree (*Chionanthus virginicus*)

Zones 4–9

12–20 feet

Sun/part shade

Fringetree is a tree for all seasons. Its delicate, white, fringelike flowers drape gracefully from the tips of its branches in spring. It is also called Old Man's Beard or Grancy Graybeard to describe these huge puffs of fluffy white. Sometimes the strappy, pure white petals are so profuse you have to look twice to be sure snow has not returned. Horticulture specialist Karen Russ reports that the botanical name Chionanthus means "snow flower." What an apt description. There are male and female trees in this dioecious species, but both have striking blooms.

After the spring floral display, glossy green leaves cover this carefree native. If a male is nearby for pollination, in late summer the female tree will produce small, dark, bluish-black fruit reminiscent of olives. Birds will clean these off the tree in a hurry. When fall arrives with its palette of brilliant colors, Fringetree usually follows suit with clear yellow leaves. It has handsome bark and usually grows as a clump tree, although it can be pruned to a single trunk. It seldom grows more than 6–10 inches in a year, a trait gardeners welcome.

PLANTING REQUIREMENTS Grow this lovely, delicate tree in moist, well-drained, slightly acidic soil. Plant it in full sun for best flowering and fall color. It is possible to transplant Fringetree if you take extreme care but it is a difficult task and the tree resents it, so it is better to plant it where you want it to grow and leave it alone. Some gardeners report deer will nibble the spring flowers, so protect it if it seems advisable.

PROPAGATION
Plant ripened seed in the fall. These take two years to germinate and subsequent growth is very slow.

Choosing native trees

As you plan your landscape, it makes sense to begin with the trees. And if you cannot use any of my suggestions, keep looking. There are many other good ones to choose from. Serviceberries are among the very first to bloom in spring. They have delicious fruit and bright red leaves to light up those delightful Indian Summer days that soothe us before the chill of winter descends.

Pagoda Dogwood and Thornless Hawthorn both provide a horizontal element in the landscape, with hiding places for nesting birds. Occasionally the Hawthorn's persistent fruit hangs on so long that it ferments, to the delight of multitudes of imbibing birds. Flowering Dogwoods and Redbuds have always been among my favorite medium-sized trees, blooming gaily in the limestone hills and along the roadsides in the Lower Midwest. I found a northern strain of Redbud here in Minnesota that has not only survived in my woods but blooms reliably each spring. The lavender-pink flowers open along the charcoal-dark branches before the heart-shaped leaves appear. Interesting seedpods clatter and clack in the breeze and in the fall the leaves become bright yellow. Gardeners in Zones 5–9 might want to try 'Lavender Twist'®, a 5-foot weeping Redbud. Like the species, it will burst forth in a blaze of yellow glory in the fall.

American Smoketree (*Cotinus obovatus*) is an incredible tree but it grows 20–30 feet tall so it needs a command position in the yard. Feathery, purple-raspberry filament hairs seem to cover the entire tree and make it look like a huge ball of rosy smoke.

Pin Cherry, Chokecherry, Prickly Ash, Mountain Maple, and Musclewood are all handsome 20–30 foot natives. So first check out my favorites above to whet your appetite, then use your imagination. You will be amazed at all the choices.

And with so many wonderful native trees available, why bother with Amur Maple and all the other common non-natives?

4.
Superb shrubs

Absolute Essentials

Sweetfern

> One of the great pleasures of gardening lies in that basic promise of a garden—that each is its owner's attempt at creating a personal paradise on earth.
>
> —Allen Paterson

When homeowners plan their landscapes, they usually begin by creating a want list. As noted in the previous chapter, the first item on that list is a usually a tree. The next item is invariably flowers. But let us not hasten to the consideration of annuals and perennials.

Are trees and flowers important? Of course, but shrubs are even more so. In fact, they may be the main component necessary to unify your home landscape. As the chapter title states, they are absolute essentials. Some will question that statement, so pause for a moment to decide whether you agree. What qualities can a shrub bring to your yard? Do they really serve any function other than to disguise the foundation of the house?

Begin by imagining a typical affordable ranch-style house set on a plot of green grass. The entire street is filled with similar houses planted squarely in the middle of each rectangle of turf grass. Except for the house, the grass stretches nearly unbroken on both sides of the street.

In this exercise let us begin by plunking a tall shade tree in the middle of the front yard. Now imagine where we might add a small space somewhere—anywhere—in that front yard, for planting flowers in full bloom that we just bought at the spring garden sale. If there is a mailbox near the street, some flowers may go there. If not, perhaps we might feel adventurous and prepare a flower bed around the new shade tree, or decide that a few flowers near the front door might be nice. (Flowers in pots do not count in this analogy, by the way. We are talking about gardens.) So once we figure that we have the right spot, we grab our spade and dig out a chunk of turf grass somewhere in the yard. Voilà! There is a garden where we can plant flowers.

Now reassess the entire picture. Is anything missing? Oh yes, maybe a few shrubs plastered in a straight line up against the house. OK, that is it. Once we buy a few shrubs at the garden center and get them planted, we are done. Right?

Wrong. Stop a moment to think about this scenario. Is this the best way to go about landscape planning?

Remember the old song by Malvina Reynolds about little boxes on the hillside that are "all made out of ticky tacky and they all look just the same." Your property need not fall into that category, but it may if you don't exercise due care. Using a little thought and a lot of imagination, it is possible to give your property distinction and character and make it unique. And you don't need an unlimited budget, either.

The easiest way to give character and uniqueness to any property, regardless of neighborhood or house style, is to create a landscape that zings. And how do we get that zing? With shrubs and with space. Step out of your comfort zone and dare to be different. Now let us walk through the process together.

Few of us put much thought into which shrubs we choose and even fewer think twice about how big these choices will become. Think about those "necessary" foundation plants crammed up against the front of most homes. Even professional landscapers are guilty of the philosophy that it has to look good *now*. We trek off to the garden center and randomly purchase a few potted shrubs that catch our eye, take them home, and plunk them in the perfectly straight, 3-foot-wide strip that runs across the front of the house. Before long we feel the need to restrain these exuberant shrubs by pruning them into balls and boxes. Several years later we attach a chain to the bumper of the family vehicle and yank them out. Then we replace them with smaller, similar ones and repeat the process.

Size matters. When you examine the tag on that cute little shrub at the garden center, pay attention to what it lists as "mature size." That tag is not kidding. Plants grow—even while you sleep. And not only do they grow *up*—they also grow *out*. It is crucial to provide these newly planted choices enough space to grow and mature without becoming unduly crowded.

And what about that pesky foundation? Homeowners should never allow shrubs to stick out their long branches and grab at guests arriving at the front door, or to block the front windows. How many times have you seen a house literally hidden behind overgrown shrubs? Or wondered, "Is *any* light getting into their living room?"

Foundation shrubs should be just that: plants to disguise the foundation and simultaneously complement the house. Begin your thought process by driving around different neighborhoods and looking at foundation plantings. You may even want to take a few photos to study when you get home and then make a simple sketch. A few tall plants at the corner of the house will soften the edges. Choose shrubs for the front of the house that will mature at less than 3 feet. Will the natural shape of one chosen plant blend with another? What kinds of groupings might complement your house, yet still provide enough space for each individual shrub to grow to maturity without crowding the shrub next to it? Will the shrubs be deciduous or evergreen? And do the evergreens have needles or leaves? What about seasonal interest: flowers, fruit, fall color? Once you determine what you really like, then it is time to choose appropriate plants. As Joseph Spence wrote in 1966, "All gardening is landscape painting."

Let us return to designing the yard as a whole. Skillful use of space can make the difference between elegant and mundane. Planting areas begin well away from the foundation. Space between plants allows them to grow naturally without becoming overcrowded. The entire planting area is pulled out from the house and often incorporates a boulder, small wall, or other feature that draws your eye from one place to the next. The edge of the garden is not stick-straight but follows a gentle curve. Planting areas come out into the yard, effectively creating a "welcome room." Shrubs are planted as single specimens, in odd groupings of 3, 5, or 7, or in large masses to make a statement. Smaller plants may be repeated throughout the garden.

A larger planting space with a variety of shrubs and flowering plants lends elegance to what would otherwise be boring and static. And getting down to fine points, you may be able to find shrubs that work well with the color of your house. For example, if it is smoky gray, find some plants with smoky gray leaves and then add a few contrasting, brightly colored perennials and annuals. Or with a plain tan or white house, a shrub with maroon foliage might be a nice addition to the green shrubs we have already chosen. Put on your thinking cap. Look at color wheels, be observant when you see plantings that intrigue you, visit a garden center or nursery to see their display plantings, or pick up a magazine. Ideas abound. Use them. It is neither necessary to reinvent the wheel, nor desirable to make your property look like every other property on the block.

What other ways can Shrubs enhance the property?

Consider the design principle that "form follows function." What functions are important to you? How can a particular type of garden or a particular type of shrub help to accomplish specific goals?

Some gardeners enjoy planting along a property line and may want to install a privacy hedge of a single shrub specimen. Determine the desired size, the qualities that are important, and figure out which species will look nice with a row of duplicates marching along the property line, either single file or in a zigzag pattern. An important consideration for a monoculture hedge is maintenance. Can it be allowed to grow naturally or will it require regular pruning? For lower maintenance, consider allowing the hedge to grow without formal pruning. It is not always necessary to use the hedge trimmers to create a flat-topped hedge with straight sides. In my thinking, shrubs growing as they do in nature are much more handsome than those rectangles we create. Maintenance for a natural shape is not difficult. Cut the largest stems to the ground every year or every other year, removing about ⅓ of the bush. For rejuvenation pruning, cut the entire shrub about 6 inches from the ground. Most shrubs will resprout and start a new plant. You need not buy new ones.

In *The Natural Habitat Garden,* Ken Druse proposes creating a biohedge. I explored this concept in my first book, *Go Native!* and declared it a winner. A biohedge is composed of a variety of native shrubs and small trees rather than just one type. Massing shrubs of different sizes and shapes can be very attractive in the back yard, either straight back or filling a corner. Along a property line this concept often works better than a monoculture hedge. Each of the specimens can be repeated along the length of the planting, just as professional designers do with a perennial border. Repetition gives order and continuity, yet a combination of types can provide seasonal interest, flowers, and fruit. Leaves may change at different times. They may be red or yellow, or remain green. A biohedge does not lend itself to formal pruning. It is planted primarily for seasonal interest and for the benefit of birds and wildlife.

Another option for a property line might be an eclectic garden filled with low-growing shrubs, tiny trees, and colorful perennials. Plants in this type of native plant border are low enough to encourage conversation between neighbors across that property line. My mom and her neighbor enjoyed the joint garden that they dug between their properties. They chose new plants at the garden center together, weeded and deadheaded flowers together, figured out how to include winter interest together, and of course, they both oohed and aahed over the beauty they had created. These two neighbors were good friends. If you enjoy friendly conversation with your neighbor you will not want to diminish that pleasure by planting a barrier. If, on the other hand, you have a troublesome neighbor, you might consider planting tall, closely spaced upright shrubs—maybe even with thorns! You can do a lot of communicating with plants.

Consider incorporating a couple of thirsty shrubs such as Buttonbush or native Prairie Rose into a rain garden to augment the colorful perennials. Rain gardens are depressions in the yard designed to collect storm runoff. Moisture-tolerant plants with deep, thirsty roots soak up the water, cleaning it in the process and preventing pollutants from running into the storm sewers. This popular new concept is discussed in chapter 11.

And of course by incorporating a few small flowering shrubs into the perennial garden you add another texture as well as winter interest when perennials are fast asleep.

I often plant a small tree or shrub where I can see it from inside the house and then, using a hose, outline a planting area that curves off from that large focal point. I have learned to go into the house before finalizing any garden. Why? Because it is important to enjoy your yard from inside as you go about your daily tasks. We all spend more time indoors than outdoors. The view from inside may mandate moving a shrub a little to the left or right. It is easier to make those adjustments before the garden is planted. So go indoors.

As you look for shrubs to add zest to your gardens, consider the planting site. Do you have full sun or dappled light? What kind of soil do you have? Is it dry or naturally moist? Will the plants you choose require additional watering?

Discussion of general planting requirements can be found in chapter 2. Particular consideration for each suggested shrub appears below under the heading Planting Requirements.

Suggested Shrubs

Here are three lists of Suggested Shrubs organized by mature size (small to medium, medium, and medium to large). Season of bloom and flower color are noted. The plants in these lists include many of my personal favorites. I chose relatively familiar native plants that are not only easy to grow, but are available at garden centers or at least from mail order sources online. Some may be easier to locate than others.

Shrub size is not an exact science and can vary greatly depending on climate and growing conditions. Many worthy native shrubs did not fit into any of these lists so I added a few of them after the plant descriptions. As I mentioned at the close of the tree chapter, if you do not find plants here that excite you, do some research. Keep looking.

Native shrubs add seasonal color including winter interest, texture, flowers, fragrance, wildlife value, and even fruit. They give a dimension to the landscape that cannot be duplicated by any other type of plant. They reduce garden maintenance because they are so self-sufficient. Shrubs are "absolute essentials" for the home landscape. And *native* shrubs are even better! Hundreds of gardenworthy native plants await you. Let the treasure hunt begin!

Small- to Medium-Sized Shrubs (2–5 feet)

Dwarf Fothergilla (*Fothergilla gardenii*)
Zones (4)5–9
18–36 inches
Blooms: late spring
White flowers
Red fall foliage
Deer resistant
Picture a small shrub laden with heavily scented, white bottlebrush flowers blooming gaily in early spring above deep purple hyacinths. Then skip forward several months and appreciate this same compact shrub glowing with wine-red and apricot-orange leaves that accent low-growing, bright yellow fall annuals or perennials. And imagine—it seldom needs pruning. How can you miss with that combination?

'Blue Mist' has blue-green foliage, but fall color is not as intense. 'KLMtwo' Beaver Creek, introduced by Roy Klehm, exhibits a tighter, more compact form. 'Windy City' has similar characteristics. Both closely resemble Dwarf Fother-gilla. Dwarf Fothergilla is hardy in Zones 5–9. Michael Dirr developed the hybrid 'Mount Airy' at the Mt. Airy Arboretum in Cincinnati, Ohio. This plant has characteristics of both Dwarf and Large Fothergilla. It becomes 4–6 feet tall.

Large Fothergilla (*F. major*) (4–12 feet), reportedly hardy to Zone 4, may need extra protection in tough winters, but with its great flowers and fantastic fall color, it is worth it. It provides an effective screen or mixed shrub border. Red Monarch™ 'KLMfifteen' (6–8 feet) literally glows with intense red foliage in the fall. The 'Mount Airy' sport 'Blue Shadow' (3–4 feet) is also hardy in Zones 4–8. The striking, waxy, steely blue-green leaves change to brilliant orange and luscious red fall foliage.

PLANTING REQUIREMENTS

Dwarf Fothergilla needs rich, moist, well-drained soil in full or part sun. The roots rot if drainage is poor. It prefers slightly acid soil; the leaves become chlorotic if the soil is too alkaline. Larger 'Mount Airy' prefers similar growing conditions, but can tolerate some dryness. Prune suckers appearing at the base of the shrub.

PROPAGATION

This shrub can be difficult to propagate by usual cutting or seeding techniques. For best results, purchase potted plants.

Leadplant (*Amorpha canescens*)

Zones 2–9
18–36 inches
Blooms: Summer
Purple flowers

Pioneers described this purple-flowering shrub in their journals as they crossed the prairies. In early to midsummer, long, 2–6 inch spikes of lavender to dark purple flowers bloom, often lasting three weeks or more. Golden-yellow anthers protrude from the ends of the tiny individual florets. As is typical of true prairie plants, Leadplant has extremely deep roots stretching 5–12 feet into the ground. Its long compound leaves are reminiscent of the pea family. Fine gray hairs make this plant look as if it is dusted with lead.

Native bees seek out the flowers. Unfortunately deer and rabbits also enjoy this protein-rich plant, so it may need protection.

PLANTING REQUIREMENTS
No particular special needs. This small shrub will tolerate any average garden soil including lean, dry sites. It flowers best in full sun and will flop and not bloom as profusely in shaded spots. It is a good choice for a rock garden.

PROPAGATION
Leadplant self-sows. Plant ripened seeds immediately for easiest propagation. Collected seeds saved for spring need both cold moist stratification and scarification.

Potentilla (*Potentilla fruticosa*)
Zone 2–7
18–40 inches
Blooms: Summer
Sun/part sun
Deer resistant

In the 1960s, we lived in Pocatello, Idaho, where Potentilla (also called Cinquefoil) grows wild in the surrounding hills. Even though it produced its familiar yellow flowers on and off throughout the growing season, the shrub was always so rangy and unkempt that I never considered it gardenworthy. But with recent hybridizing efforts, multiple hybrids and cultivars bloom their heads off most of the summer. Potentilla is readily available for purchase and comes in a wide range of colors and sizes. It has small, gray-green leaves but no fall color.

Cultivars include white flowered 'Abbotswood', creamy white 'McKay's White', yellow 'Coronation Triumph', lemon-yellow 'Gold Drop', and pale yellow 'Primrose Beauty'. 'Pink Beauty' has semi-double pale pink flowers. 'Mango Tango' is an attention-grabber with deep yellow flowers sporting an orangey-red center. Most cultivars are 2–3 feet tall, although the arching, upright branches of golden-yellow 'Goldfinger' can stretch to 4 feet.

Potentilla is the only known food source for the Cinquefoil Copper butterfly.

PLANTING REQUIREMENTS

Plant in average, well-drained garden soil in full sun for best blooms. Potentilla prefers a dry planting site and alkaline soil. If it gets that typical rangy look after two to three years, just cut it to the ground and it will dutifully sprout back into a compact shape.

PROPAGATION

Potentilla cuttings are easy to root. Sow ripened seeds outdoors in fall. Germination is fairly reliable.

Native Spiraea (*Spiraea* spp.)

Zones 3–8

2–4 feet

Blooms: Late summer

Deer resistant

Rain garden

Most gardeners are familiar with overused Japanese Spirea, commonly chosen for foundation plantings. Did you know that a few native Spiraeas work as well or better?

Birchleaf Spiraea (*Spiraea betulifolia*) grows as a compact, rounded 2–3-foot shrub and is the earliest of these three native spiraeas to bloom. Flat clusters of fuzzy white flowers appear in May and June. This species has colorful fall leaves of orange, yellow, and burgundy. The cultivar 'Tor' has burgundy-red fall color and is more compact than the species. It needs consistently moist soil.

Steeplebush (*S. tomentosa*) gets its common name from the tall, rosy-pink, steeple-like flowers that bloom in late summer. Blooms can be 4–8 inches long and appear on new growth. This plant blooms for nearly a month; deadheading will extend the bloom period. The backs of the leaves of Steeplebush are soft and fuzzy, described by its botanical name, *tomentosa*, meaning hairy or woolly. Another common name, Hard Hack, refers to its tough stems. Steeplebush is another suckering shrub that likes moist spots. This 2–3-foot shrub can be used in foundation plantings or along walkways and is a good choice for rain gardens. Prune suckers to show off the reddish-orange exfoliating bark. Autumn leaves are yellow. It is the larval host of the Columbia Silkmoth.

Meadowsweet (*S. alba* aka *S. latifolia*) (sometimes also identified as *S. alba* var. *latifolia*) is another native spiraea with fuzzy white pyramidal flowers that also bloom in mid to late summer. It grows 2–4 feet tall and has shiny green leaves.

PLANTING REQUIREMENTS
Native spiraeas prefer full sun and moist to average, slightly acidic soil that is well drained. They will also grow in part shade, but the seasonal colors may diminish with less light.

PROPAGATION
The best way to propagate these native spiraeas is by rooting softwood cuttings in early summer.

New Jersey Tea (*Ceanothus americanus*)
Zones 4–9
3–4 feet
Blooms: Early summer
White flowers
Deer resistant

New Jersey Tea has a history. Colonists used its dried leaves to make tea, especially in 1773 when they were protesting Britain's tea tax. It was called red root by pioneer farmers who found it difficult to plow the soil in prairie areas where these gnarly, deeply rooted plants grew. This small compact shrub is loaded with fluffy, creamy white flower clusters in late spring. It fixes nitrogen in the soil. Just imagine all that natural "fertilizer" each time there is a thunderstorm. The yellow-green fall leaf color is nothing to get excited about, but it is worth planting for its small, compact growth habit and its attraction to butterflies. In fact, many butterfly enthusiasts call it a "must have" plant. This is a larval food host for the Mottled Duskywing and the Spring and Summer Azure butterflies.

This shrub has two major challenges. Rabbits cannot resist nibbling the new shoots, so plant protection is in order, especially in early spring. It does not seem to be as much of a problem later in the season. Maybe they find enough to eat elsewhere. And the second challenge? Buying it. Unfortunately, it may be difficult to find. I tried to purchase it when we first moved to Minnesota in 2003. The garden center staff told me they had stocked it for a couple of years, but it did not sell well and was no longer available. But it appears to be readily available on the Web or through plant catalogs such as Prairie Nursery in Westfield, Wisconsin. Just go hunting. And be a squeaky wheel at the local garden center. Maybe if enough native plant enthusiasts squeak, more natives will find their way onto the garden center plant tables.

PLANTING REQUIREMENTS

Plant in average, well-drained soil in full sun to part shade. If it begins to look rangy, give it a rejuvenation haircut in late winter or early spring, hard-pruning it nearly to the ground. Take a lesson from the pioneers and realize that this is a difficult plant to move once it is established, so plant it where it can remain.

PROPAGATION

New Jersey Tea is not easy to propagate because it is difficult to collect the seeds. The capsules explode, throwing seeds all over. Few germinate. Softwood cuttings taken from new growth in early spring may be the best option.

Snowberry (*Symphoricarpos* spp.)

Zones 2–7

2–4 feet

Blooms: Early to mid summer

Deer resistant

Rain garden

Snowberries lack fall color, but make up for it with a nice display of interesting fruit that remains on the naked branches into the winter until the birds find it. I enjoy growing several different Snowberry shrubs on the sides of the rain garden. Coralberry, also called Indian Currant (*S. orbiculatus*), produces bright coral-red berries that sparkle in the fall and winter landscape. These profuse berries march up and down the naked branches and last as long as the birds allow it. Coralberry grows 3–4 feet tall in my garden.

Snowberry (*S. albus*) is a tad taller, reaching 4–6 feet in my sunny spot. Familiar clusters of fat, white snowberries tuck in among the blue-gray leaves and continue to cling to the naked branches after the leaves drop in the fall. I found a variegated cultivar (*S. albus variegatus*) advertised on the Web. It has a narrow, creamy white margin on the green leaves with the usual half-inch white snowberries.

My favorites are the pink Snowberries. Little 'Hancock' (*S.* × *chenaultii*) seldom exceeds 2 feet. The delicate pink clusters of berries covering the stiff stalks, persisting late into the season, are irresistible. Occasionally I prune off two or three branches laden with berries, bring them into the house, and add a few flowers from the florist or grocery store. Just seeing that little bouquet can lift my spirits and brighten a gray wintry day. *S.* × *doorenbosii,* a hybrid of *S. albus laevitigatus* and *S.* × *chenaultii,* has been responsible for several pretty pink cultivars. 'Candy Sensation', also called 'Kolmcan', has clear, candy-pink berries in September. It grows 24–36 inches tall. 'Marleen'® produces dark purplish-pink berries and blue-green summer foliage with pale gray-green leaf backs. Bright pink 'Amethyst'™ berries really stand out. But then I love anything pink.

PLANTING REQUIREMENTS
Plant in average to moist, well-drained soil in full sun. Space the plants to allow ample air circulation and discourage mildew. Cut close to the ground every three to four years to maintain a compact bushy form and encourage heavier fruiting. Remove suckers as necessary.

PROPAGATION
Coralberry is an arching shrub. Tips touching the ground will root. Root soft-wood or hardwood cuttings in early to midsummer.

Medium Shrubs 4–8 feet

Serviceberry (*Amelanchier alnifolia* 'Regent')
Zones 3–9
3–5 feet
Blooms: Spring
White flowers
Red fall foliage
Deer resistant

Serviceberries, also called Juneberry and Shadbush, are beautiful small trees and shrubs with unsurpassed seasonal interest. However, their mature height of 15–25 feet is really too large for most small landscapes.

Saskatoon Serviceberry (*Amelanchier alnifolia*) is the smallest. It also has the best tasting fruit.

Choose the compact *A. alnifolia* 'Regent' for small spaces rather than the species. This seed-propagated selection generally grows about 5 feet tall. In spring, the gardener will be rewarded with upright clusters of small, white flowers appearing before the rounded sawtooth green leaves. In summer, abundant green berries hang thickly from the branches. These turn rose, then ripen to rich bluish-black. Make delicious jelly from these dark, juicy berries, dry the fruit like raisins for trail mix, or just nibble a few. Animals and birds love the berries too, so there may be a race for the prize. Native Americans crushed the dried berries and added them to dried meat and fat to make pemmican.

In fall, shades of bright orange-yellow and brilliant red create a bright spot in the landscape. The bark color ranges from reddish-brown to dark gray.

Hummingbirds and Spring Azure butterflies relish the sweet flower nectar. It is a larval host plant for the Swallowtail butterfly. Serviceberries are valuable wildlife plants, providing food and shelter for over 40 species.

PLANTING REQUIREMENTS
Native to the Great Plains, this shrub prefers well-drained soil. It is not fussy about moisture and will accept some drought. Although it will tolerate some shade, for best flowering and fruiting site it in a sunny spot. Remove suckers and provide good air circulation to prevent mildew.

PROPAGATION
Divide in early spring, dig and transplant rooted suckers. Scarify ripened seed and plant immediately or store in refrigerator and plant in spring. Purchase cultivars and hybrids.

Smooth Hydrangea (*Hydrangea arborescens*)
Zones 3–9
3–5 feet
Blooms: Early summer
Rain garden
Well-known 'Annabelle' reliably produces huge 8–10-inch clusters of sterile white flowers that dry to buff tan in the fall. Cut these dried flowers for a winter bouquet. Because the flowers tend

to flop after a heavy rain, some gardeners plant two or three close together to support one another. The cultivar 'Incrediball' has even larger white flowers with stronger stems to prevent flopping. It grows 4–5 feet tall. If you prefer smaller white flowers, choose 'Grandiflora' with 6–8-inch flower heads.

Pink is the new buzz on the hydrangea scene. 'Invincibelle Spirit' has lovely, large, dusty-rose blooms and grows 4–5 feet tall. Partial proceeds from each sale are donated to the Breast Cancer Research Foundation. A reblooming pink form of 'Annabelle' named 'Bella Anna', also known as 'PIHA-1', with even stronger stems, was developed by Michael Dirr as part of the Endless Summer series. The first dark pink flowers bloom in early summer. Then in late summer or early fall a second flush of pink flowers blooms on the new growth of this exciting 3–6-foot hydrangea. This shrub is worth searching for.

PLANTING REQUIREMENTS
Hydrangeas prefer well-drained soil and dislike wet roots. Northern gardeners have better success with full sun, while those in the hot, humid southern states should provide afternoon shade. Extra water is appreciated, especially in hot weather or when the soil begins to get dry. Cut suckers when they appear.

PROPAGATION
The easiest way to propagate hydrangeas is with a softwood tip cut from a nonflowering branch. Cut below at least 3 nodes, remove the leaves from the bottom nodes and then cut each existing leaf in half. Treat with rooting compound if you have some. I cut a liter pop bottle and inverted it over a flowerpot filled with dampened sand, creating a mini-greenhouse. Voilà! The hydrangea rooted.

Virginia Sweetspire (*Itea virginica*)
Zones 5–9
3–5 feet
Blooms: Early to midsummer
Full sun to part shade
William Cullina writes, "Kitten-tail flower spikes arch away from the mound of foliage like trailing fireworks." Wow. Not even a good photograph can top that description. In late fall, leaves in full sun turn brilliant burgundy-red.

With less light, the leaves develop softer shadings of yellow, green, red, and orange. The long-lasting fall color alone is worth the price of this shrub.

The familiar cultivar 'Henry's Garnet' is the easiest to find commercially. It seldom exceeds 3 feet and has larger flowers than the species. Its dark green leaves change to intense shades of scarlet in the fall, persisting until late in the season. Several websites recommend this introduction as a good alternative to non-native Burning Bush. For a smaller version, look for 'Little Henry'. Several other cultivars are available including 'Merlot', with intense wine-red fall foliage, but none gets higher marks than 'Henry's Garnet'.

Sweetspire leafs out late in the summer but do not dig it out. Give it time and it will soon reappear in all its glory.

PLANTING REQUIREMENTS

The species thrives on tough love. Plant it in average, well-drained soil that is more dry than moist. Cultivars seem to appreciate more consistent moisture and some can tolerate fairly wet sites as long as the soil is well drained. For best color, plant Itea where it can get lots of sunlight. Then watch it flourish in your garden.

PROPAGATION

Root green-leafed hardwood cuttings in late summer or fall. Seeding is tedious and not always successful.

Summersweet (*Clethra alnifolia*)

Zones 3–9

3–8 feet tall

Blooms: Mid- to late summer

Salt tolerant

Deer resistant

Summersweet demands close proximity to people. I have three of these extremely fragrant shrubs near my patio. For nearly a month every summer I enjoy the wonderful fragrance that the delicate flowers exude. Butterflies and hummingbirds adore Clethra, constantly seeking out the pink or white flower racemes to enjoy the sweet nectar. Summersweet flowers appear on new growth so spring pruning to remove any winter-killed branches is not a major issue. Glossy green leaves cover the small compact shrub for most of the growing season and change to bright, clear yellow in the fall, lighting up the landscape. It is a wonderful addition to the native plant garden. Plant it around the porch or patio, use it near the front of a border garden, as a foundation shrub, in a group, or alone as a specimen. My shrubs grow slowly and invariably leaf out later in my Minnesota garden than I expect. Clethra reportedly suckers. Mine has not.

'Hummingbird' grows 3 feet tall and flowers more heavily than the species. It has a tidy compact form. The white flowers of 'Sixteen Candles' stand upright as the name suggests. 'Rosea' has dark pink buds that open as soft pink flowers. The pink fades to white as they age. 'Pink Spires' and 'Ruby Spice' both remain pink. For larger flowers, look for 'Vanilla Spice'. 'Compacta', chosen by Longwood Gardens as the best dwarf cultivar after a 7-year Clethra trial, won the 2010 Gold Medal Award from the Pennsylvania Horticultural Society. Fall-blooming 'September Beauty' will extend the clethra fragrance. Gardeners looking for a tiny, compact Clethra can try 'Sugartina'™ (aka 'Crystaline'). It seldom tops 30 inches.

PLANTING REQUIREMENTS
Plant in moist, humus-rich, well-drained soil in full sun or partial shade. It dislikes drought and appreciates additional moisture when temperatures spike in summer. Remove winter-killed wood in late winter or early spring. Cut leggy growth to the ground to rejuvenate and promote new compact growth.

PROPAGATION
Dig and transplant rooted suckers. Root cuttings in late spring or early summer. This plant is easy to propagate and new seedlings grow quickly.

Ninebark (*Physocarpus opulifolius*)
Zones 2–8
5–8 feet ('Little Devil', 3–4 feet)
Pink flowers
Blooms: Late spring to early summer
Ninebark is the shrub that Michael Dirr insists "needs a bulldozer for removal." I planted three small potted specimens of the cultivar 'Diablo' along our stucco garage wall. They quickly outgrew the space. Yes, they provide a vivid contrasting color, and in late spring pretty pink flowers peep out among the burgundy-red leaves.

However, their arching branches lean out across the grass, with the tips nearly touching our property line. This makes a casual walk down the hill more difficult than necessary. And try mowing! Hard pruning does little for the pleasing natural shape and only temporarily curtails Ninebark's exuberant spirit. I admit I planted the wrong plant in the wrong place. So now what?

Enter 'Little Devil'. Dr. David Zlesak, Professor of Horticulture at the University of Wisconsin–River Falls, named his new hybrid Ninebark after his mom (*P. opulifolius* 'Donna May'). Bailey Nursery chose this cross between 'Diablo' and the species as one of its First Editions® introductions. 'Little Devil' exhibits many of the same pleasing 'Diablo' characteristics including glossy burgundy leaves and pink flowers, but only grows 3–4 feet high and wide. It is disease resistant and maintains a compact upright form. With this growth habit, 'Little Devil' is an excellent foundation planting. Add it to a perennial garden or plant it close to a walkway. It even works in a container surrounded by contrasting annuals. Invite this cute little devil into your yard. You will enjoy his company. 'Coppertina' and 'Summer Wine' are also good cultivars.

PLANTING REQUIREMENTS
Ninebark is not fussy; it will grow in sun or shade and dry or moist, rich or lean soil as long as it is well drained.

PROPAGATION
Propagate by rooting softwood cuttings from new growth in spring, or plant ripened seeds in fall. Purchase patented cultivars.

Viburnum spp.
Zones 3–8
3–8 feet
Blooms: Late spring
White flowers
Full sun/part shade
Deer resistant
Rain garden
Arrowwood Viburnum (*V. dentatum*) is one of my favorite viburnums. 'Autumn Jazz', a Chicagoland Grows cultivar, displays more vibrant fall color than the species, with apricot-orange, red, and golden-yellow shouting out a magnificent concert of color. But there is another reason to grow the cultivar.

Rabbits relentlessly mow the species off just above ground level, effectively performing rejuvenation pruning nearly every winter. 'Autumn Jazz' must not be as palatable because they never touch those shrubs even though I have the two types interspersed. I also grow 'Chicago Lustre' (aka 'Synnestvedt') with glossy green summer leaves that turn purple and gold in the fall. Other Arrowwood cultivars include 'Northern Burgundy' (aka 'Morton') and 'Cardinal' with multiple shades of red. Arrowwood has white flowers in spring, black fruits, and is the larval food for several moths and the Spring Azure butterfly.

'Blue Muffin'® (*V. dentatum* 'Christom') is a real winner for the garden or shrub border. It matures at 3–5 feet and when this cute little shrub is loaded with its color-crayon blue fruits, it is a spectacular sight. It needs another Arrowwood shrub nearby for pollination and good fruit production so why not plant a half-pint version? Roy Klehm's 4-foot 'Little Joe', aka 'KLMseventeen', is the perfect choice.

Downy Arrowwood (*V. rafinesquianum*) is smaller than Arrowwood. It has a dense, compact form, white flowers, blue-black fruits, and wine-red fall foliage. It will thrive in either acid or alkaline soil as long as it is well drained. Once established, it is relatively drought tolerant. It prefers sun, but will accept part shade. It is recommended for rain gardens.

American Cranberrybush (*V. opulus* var. *americanum*) was formerly called *V. trilobum* to denote the three-lobed leaves. The new nomenclature includes var. *americanum* to differentiate it from the European species *V. opulus*. This popular viburnum grows 8–12 feet tall with large clusters of white flowers in spring. Plant it in bright sunshine to get the best rich burgundy fall color and the biggest clusters of juicy red fruit. Birds will devour these berries as soon as they ripen, so if you have any desire to make jelly, get out there fast.

Heavier-fruiting cultivars include 'Andrews', 'Hahs', and 'Wentworth'. I have 'Wentworth' and can attest to its incredible fruiting capability. But so far I have never beaten the birds to the prize. 'Phillips' is a nice dwarf-sized cultivar. 'Redwing' has lots of red beginning in early spring with red-tinged foliage and red petioles. In fall it sports red leaves and red fruit. So if you are a lover of red, this may be your best bet. This is the shrub that Bailey Nursery has developed into a tree form described in chapter 3. 'Bailey Compact', 3–6 feet tall, is one of the best compact fruit producing selections. 'Alfredo' is 5–6 feet tall with a very dense growth habit. Monrovia offers *V. trilobum* 'Compactum', hardy in Zones 2–7, which grows 6 feet tall and wide. But be careful when you look for 'Compactum' if you are looking for a *native* selection. There is also a Korean Spice Viburnum (*V. carlesii*) named 'Compactum', so check the botanical name before you buy.

Bright red autumn leaves of Maple Leaf Viburnum (*V. acerifolium*) absolutely pop in the fall landscape. This little shrub naturalizes in eastern woodlands, but enjoys full sun too. It has delicate white flowers in spring; tiny, round, blue-black berries; and maple-like leaves. It only grows 3–6 feet tall. Maple Leaf Viburnum will sucker, but if you don't want a small colony of these, prune the suckers when they appear. It is hardy in Zones 3–8.

Possumhaw Viburnum (*V. nudum*) stands 5–12 feet tall and is hardy in Zones 5–9. It features maroon fall foliage and deep blue fruits. The unique fruits of 'Winterthur' begin as bubblegum pink and mature to blueberry blue. This 6-foot cultivar has brilliant maroon-red fall foliage and is a showstopper. Plant another viburnum nearby to provide cross-pollination for good fruit production. 'Brandywine' produces pink and blue berries growing together on the same cluster. How about that for a great conversation piece! 'Count Pulaski' grows 5–7 feet tall. Southern Possumhaw (*V. nudum* var. *nudum*) is hardy in Zones 6–9. Northern Witherod (*V. nudum* var. *cassinoides*) hardy in Zones 2–8, is taller, maturing 8–12 feet tall.

Highbush Cranberry (*V. edule*) can also be found as Squashbush, Squashberry, or Moosewood Viburnum. Hardy in Zones 2–7, *V. edule* is similar to the more familiar Cranberrybush (*V. trilobum*) with 3-lobed leaves, but the leaves are smaller and the flowers are less showy.

Rusty Blackhaw, also called Blue Haw (*V. rufidulum*) is hardy in Zone 5–9. It is drought tolerant and has leathery, dark green foliage. The foliage changes to burgundy red in fall. This species is not as showy as some of the other viburnum species.

Blackhaw (*V. prunifolium*) *and* Nannyberry (*V. lentago*) are described in the previous chapter on native trees. Each can also be grown as a shrub.

PLANTING REQUIREMENTS

Viburnums are very shade tolerant, but for best flower and fruit production and the most vibrant fall color, plant in full sun. These shrubs can handle average, nearly neutral soil in wet or dry conditions, but the soil needs to be well drained.

PROPAGATION

In early summer, cut and root new sucker growth that has not produced flowers. When roots form, transplant into pots to grow stronger before planting in the garden.

Large Shrubs (Maturing over 9 feet)

Chokeberry (*Aronia* spp.)
Zones 3–10
3–10 feet
Blooms: Spring
White flowers
Deer resistant
Rain garden

Dainty white flowers bloom in early spring, but the real reason to grow Chokeberry is its vivid fall color. Most gardeners are familiar with Burning Bush (*Euonymus alatus*), the Asian escape artist that takes over wild spaces. Instead, choose native Chokeberry, either Red or Black. Both have varied seasonal interest, brilliant fall leaves, and are relatively well behaved and slow-growing.

Red Chokeberry (*A. arbutifolia*) is the tallest at 5–10 feet. Pretty white spring flowers become fat, juicy red berries in midsummer, persisting to fall. Birds and wildlife nibble them, but if you try to eat them raw, they taste awful—hence the common name. But oh, what yummy jam and jelly you can make. 'Brilliantissima' is more compact than the species with brighter colored fruit and even more vivid red leaves in the fall.

Black Chokeberry (*A. melanocarpa*), Zones 3–9, grows 3–6 feet tall. Its profuse berries are black. Otherwise seasonal characteristics are nearly identical to Red Chokeberry. I have this shrub in my perennial garden and it has been well behaved with no untoward suckering or high-maintenance pruning needed. Glossy Black Chokeberry ('Elata') has glossy green leaves and only grows 4 feet tall. May-blooming 'Iroquois Beauty' is 2–3 feet tall. A 2012 introduction named 'Autumn Black Magic' makes a wonderful hedge or a handsome specimen. It can also be used as erosion control on a hillside or serve as part of a native plant border. It is loaded with those black berries that appear after a fantastic spring flower display. The fall color is spectacular. Chokeberries will grow in wet or dry, sun or shade and are beautiful in all seasons. They are good shrubs for a rain garden.

PLANTING REQUIREMENTS

Plant in average, well-drained soil in full sun. Remove suckers to prevent this plant from getting overly rambunctious. Some cultivars are less prone to profuse suckering.

PROPAGATION

Plant ripened seed in fall or cold stratify in the refrigerator for spring planting. Root softwood cuttings in early summer.

Northern Bayberry (*Myrica pensylvanica*)

Zones 3–7

3–10 feet

Deer resistant

Salt tolerant

Rain garden

Herb gardeners enjoy growing Northern Bayberry for the small, grayish-white berries they harvest to make bayberry candles or soap. This shrub has male and female bushes, so plant at least one male to provide pollination. You will have to hunt for the berries because they hide under the new growth. Bayberry creates a good hedge, controls erosion on hillsides, and thrives in a rain garden. 'Morton' is a 4–5-foot female clone from the Morton Arboretum.

PLANTING REQUIREMENTS

Prefers slightly acidic, well-drained soil in full sun to part shade. Will tolerate salt and occasional drought. This moisture-lover appreciates being mulched, but poorly drained soil can cause root rot. It dislikes being fertilized. Cut suckers unless you want it to create a large mass.

PROPAGATION

Dig a rooted sucker to transplant in early spring, root softwood cuttings in early summer, plant ripened seed immediately, or cold stratify for spring planting.

Red Twig Dogwood (*Cornus sericea*)

Zones 3–8

6–9 feet

Blooms: Late spring to early summer

White flowers

Deer resistant

Rain garden

My neighbor and I share those ugly green utility property-line boxes that hold the electrical stuff for TV, cable, and telephone that homeowners need in order to survive. Most of us try to screen these necessaries with plantings. A former owner ringed our small utility boxes with Red Twig Dogwoods and I have to admit they do the job, especially in winter when the red stems glow against our Minnesota snow. However, they are the 6–9-foot variety, so we have to prune regularly to keep them neat and tidy. Some recommend cutting them to the ground to keep them in check, but we tried that once and it took a couple years before the shrubs recovered enough to be a decent size. Now we just remove the largest stems and prune the rest of the branches to an appropriate height. This shrub is also known as Red Osier Dogwood and Red Stem Dogwood. As long as you designate *Cornus sericea,* you will have the right plant.

For homeowners who love brightly colored stems of red or yellow in the winter, consider choosing a smaller cultivar. 'Firedance'™ (*C. sericea*), another name for 'Bailadeline', grows 3–4 feet tall. Its compact growth habit is a joy for "take it easy" gardeners who dislike constant pruning chores. In spring it is covered with white flower clusters followed by white berries. Fall leaves are an intense scarlet-plum and the naked, bright red winter stems never disappoint. It is similar to the 5–6-foot University of Minnesota introduction 'Isanti', but a little smaller and more compact. Tolerant of wet sites, it is a good choice for a rain garden. It also is a great foundation plant that does not take over the world. It is hardy in Zones 2–7.

Lovers of yellow stems can plant Yellow Twig Dogwood (*C. sericea* 'Flaviramea'). It is a 10-footer, but tends to be more wimpy than the Red Twig variety.

There is a cultivar of my favorite Gray Dogwood (*C. racemosa*) named 'Muszam' aka 'Muskingum'®. This slow grower has the familiar red-stemmed white berries and burgundy fall leaves, but it is stoloniferous and can eventually cover a hillside that needs erosion control. It only grows 2–3 feet tall but spreads 4–5 feet wide.

PLANTING REQUIREMENTS
Plant in average, well-drained garden soil in full sun for best seasonal color. Can tolerate some drought.

PROPAGATION
Cut several of last year's red branches in early spring and put them in a vase with about 6 inches of water covering the base of each branch. Enjoy them on your kitchen counter in a spot with fairly bright light but not direct sunlight. Like a pussy willow whip, some of these red or yellow-stemmed dogwoods may sprout roots. Pot rooted stems and plant them outdoors later in the spring.

Oakleaf Hydrangea (*Hydrangea quercifolia*)
Zones 5–9

4–6 feet

Blooms: Late spring to midsummer

As a resident of Zone 4 Minnesota, I admit to lusting after anything that likes warmer planting zones. A case in point is Oakleaf Hydrangea (*Hydrangea quercifolia*). I first saw this marvelous shrub at a friend's home in Indianapolis and promptly fell in love with it. It grows 4–6 feet tall and wide. Its large, oak-like leaves change to rich tones of bronze, purple, and crimson in the fall. In winter the bark is a handsome deep brown. But oh, the flowers! The flowers are definitely the stars of this shrub. Huge, 6–12-inch-long pointed clusters of pure white cover the new leaves in late spring and last into summer. When you come around the corner on the path and see them, you have to catch your breath. These lovely flowers age to a pale pink and finally dry to tan. Bring them inside for dried arrangements, or leave them outside on the bush for continued winter interest.

Michael Dirr's 'Alice' is even larger and more impressive with more and bigger flowers. Several gardening websites describe it as BIG and ROBUST. 'Snowflake' actually has double blossoms. These 15-inch panicles begin bright white and then change to a pink and dusty rose that gives a two-toned effect on these striking, long-lasting flowers. Autumn leaves are deep burgundy-red. 'Sike's Dwarf' is a 2–3-foot miniature copy of 'Alice'. 'Pee Wee' is 3–4 feet tall but has smaller leaves and flowers and less tendency to sucker.

PLANTING REQUIREMENTS
Plant in consistently moist, well-drained soil in full sun to part shade. Keep shrubs in full sun well watered, especially during the heat of summer.

PROPAGATION
Root non-blooming softwood cuttings in early summer.

Winterberry Holly (*Ilex verticillata*)
Zones 3–9
3–8 (12) feet (varies)
Blooms: Summer
Deer resistant
Rain garden

Unlike American Holly (*Ilex opaca*) and English Holly (*I. aquifolium*), those familiar evergreens so popular for Christmas decorating, Winterberry Holly does not have the deeply toothed leaves, nor is it evergreen. But don't despair. The leaves during the growing season are glossy and dark green. After the leaves fall, the bright red berries look even more spectacular, providing a show in winter when we all yearn for color.

All holly species are dioecious. Plant at least one male within 30–40 feet of female shrubs to ensure production of berries. Timing for effective pollination is critical, so choose a male that blooms at the same time as your females. 'Jim Dandy' is early (E); 'Raritan Chief' mid-season (M); 'Apollo' late (L), and 'Southern Gentleman' (LL) very late. If you're not sure, plant several different males. To identify a shrub in bloom as male or female, look at the small flowers that bloom in spring. Female flowers have a little knob in the center known as the pistil. Male flowers send up several hairlike filaments with a tiny pouch on top of each that holds the pollen and is recognized as the anther. (These parts are readily identifiable in the familiar Easter Lily. If you carefully pinch out the bright yellow anthers, you will trick the flower into believing it has not been pollinated and must bloom longer).

My favorite winterberry cultivar is little 'Red Sprite', also known as 'Nana'. Only 2–4-feet tall, it grows in a rounded, compact shape, and does this beauty ever hang on to its profuse bright red fruit! 'Red Sprite' lights up the gloom of winter, so plant it where you can see it from inside the house. 'Afterglow' produces reddish-orange fruits on dense, upright branches that grow 3–6 feet tall. The favorite pollinator of both 'Red Sprite' and 'Afterglow' is little 5-foot 'Jim Dandy'.

If you want orange-tone berries in the fall, 'Winter Gold' will fill the bill. 'Winter Gold' needs a late to very late season pollinator such as 'Southern Gentleman'. Its leaves change from glossy green in autumn to striking shades of yellow, salmon, and apricot before they drop. Both are relatively tall cultivars, maturing at 6–8 feet.

Gardeners who love variegated leaves should look for 'Sunsplash'. The leaves are literally splashed with patches of white, gold, and green, creating an unequaled conversation piece. A fantastic fall show of bright reddish-orange berries is guaranteed as long as 'Jim Dandy' is nearby.

PLANTING REQUIREMENTS

Plant in moist, average to rich soil in full sun. Winterberry Holly will tolerate wet sites and poor drainage, but also thrives in normal, well-drained soil.

PROPAGATION

Root cuttings in early summer or plant seeds. Like the seeds of Jack-in-the-Pulpit, holly seeds are encased in soft pulp. Place in a sieve under warm running water and rub to remove the pulp. Plant near the mother shrub immediately after cleaning if you want to "take it easy," or put the seeds in a plastic zip-lock bag with vermiculite in a warm place for 2–3 months. Then cold stratify in the refrigerator for up to 4 months. The seed can take 1–3 years to germinate. Suit yourself, but personally, I would rather just buy the plants!

Elderberry (*Sambucus canadensis*)

Zones 3–9
Blooms: Summer
White flowers
5–12 feet
Deer resistant

Elderberry, also called American Elder, grows abundantly along roadsides. In early summer, clusters of frothy white flowers cover the green-leaved shrubs, followed by deep black fruits. These fruits are devoured by birds and wildlife and occasionally gathered by people in the know to make jams, jellies, tasty drinks, and wine. Elderberry is still considered a rangy shrub, only suitable for the wilder areas of suburban gardens, but with annual or semiannual rejuvenation pruning, it can actually become a respectable city dweller. And Japanese Beetles pay no attention to it. Now that is a plus!

You will often see reference to fancy elderberry cultivars including some with lacy, nearly black leaves. Unfortunately most of those have originated from *Sambucus nigra,* a European species. There is one popular cultivar of our native Elderberry called 'Aurea' with golden leaves and bright red fruit. It needs full sun to really develop the yellow leaf color. It grows 6–12 feet tall and is hardy in Zones 3–9. For heavy fruit production, choose 'York' and 'Adams'. 'Laciniata' has finely cut leaves, providing good textural interest to the landscape.

American Red Elderberry (*S. pubens*) grows 6–12 feet tall. This native blooms earlier in the spring. Airy white flower clusters burst forth in May followed by large bunches of brilliant red berries prized by birds and gobbled by their young babies. Don't eat these raw. Instead, gather the black fruits of our familiar roadside elderberries (*S. canadensis*) to make those familiar tasty treats. If you must taste the tempting red berries, be sure to cook them thoroughly. Or better yet, remember those red berries "are for the birds!" Just leave them on the bush for the wildlings.

PLANTING REQUIREMENTS
Elderberries tolerate a wide variety of soils, but like moist or wet, well-drained soil best. They can tolerate some drought once established. Maintenance includes regular rejuvenation pruning to 6–8 feet to keep this shrub tidy. Prune suckers at the base.

Witch Hazel (*Hamamelis* spp.)
Zones 4–8
Blooms: See description
Yellow flowers
Deer resistant
Rain garden
Every gardener needs the promise of spring, and what could be better than looking out the window onto a wintry landscape and spying the bright yel-

low confetti flowers of a winter blooming Vernal Witch Hazel (*Hamamelis vernalis*). The sight of a shrub loaded with these small rays of sunshine is guaranteed to make your day. I have taken photographs of this bush in full bloom while standing knee deep in snow. Because outside temperatures can be cold in February and March, the delicate flowers last and last, sometimes for over two months.

Speed through the seasons to discover the other Witch Hazel (*H. virginiana* L.) putting on its late fall show. Narrow strappy yellow flowers hide shyly under masses of apricot-gold leaves. Delight in the quiet beauty of this Witch Hazel, one of the last shrubs to brighten the fall landscape before winter begins in earnest. This shrub can become 8–20 feet tall, whereas its season-awakening sibling rarely exceeds 6–12 feet.

As an impressionable child of five, I remember following my Uncle Alvin behind my grandmother's house where he cut a forked branch from a Witch Hazel shrub growing there. He told me it was a magic witching stick that would point to Grandma's well. Holding the Y pointed out and slightly down, he walked around the back yard. When he got to the well, the branch suddenly bent and dipped toward the ground. I was wide-eyed and peered back fearfully at the magical witch bush, but nope. No witch to be seen.

PLANTING REQUIREMENTS
Witch Hazels enjoy moist, well-drained planting sites in full to part sun. I had the winter bloomer near the edge of our back yard at our home in Indiana. It caught the sun just right and left fantastic shadow traceries on the snow late in the afternoon.

PROPAGATION
Softwood cuttings taken in late spring or early summer might work, but this is not the easiest plant to propagate. You may find a seedling to transplant or, easier yet, just purchase the shrub.

Are there other native Shrubs to consider?

When I began researching this book, I searched for unusual small native shrubs to include. I was fascinated by information on Sweetfern (*Comptonia peregrina*) including a 1996 article published in the Arnold Arboretum's journal, *Arnoldia,* detailing attempts to propagate it. The author, Peter Del

Tredici, included this commentary from Henry D. Thoreau's journal entry of January 1860: "Those little groves of sweet-fern still thickly leafed, whose tops now rise above the snow, are an interesting warm brown-red now, like the reddest oak leaves." Imagine having a shrub in your garden that resembles a fern. Native Americans used Sweetfern medicinally and it remains popular with modern herbalists. Fresh or dried leaves thrown into the bonfire reportedly repel mosquitoes. Steeping the leaves in hot water makes a nice tea. How could I resist those credentials? I was hooked. I promptly asked Jean to render this drawing.

However, later research revealed that Sweetfern is not the easiest plant to grow in town or suburbia and may be next to impossible to purchase. It is more suited for wild, sandy, acidic sites and is probably better at stopping soil erosion than providing focal points in gardens. Still, you may want to know enough about it to identify it in the wild. Hardy in Zones 3–7, Sweetfern grows from 6 inches to about 3 or 4 feet tall. In early spring, small white flowers bloom and later these become small brown edible nutlets. One source calls them a "tasty nibble." Sweetfern can grow in either sun or part shade. It tolerates drought in shady spots, but needs more moisture in full sun. This shrub fixes nitrogen in the soil and prefers a well-drained planting spot. Researchers report that successful seeding is difficult. Best results may be obtained by planting green seeds before they are fully ripe. Established plants are deep rooted and difficult to divide or transplant, but some report success harvesting rooted suckers in spring. So there you have it. And if you successfully grow this fascinating fern-like shrub, let me know!

Bog Birch (*Betula pumila* var. *glandulifera*) is also called Dwarf Birch. It is hardy in Zones 2–9, grows 3–6 feet tall and wide, and suckers heavily. In a particularly favorable location, it can shoot up to 12–15 feet. It is especially suited to wild, wet areas but is not recommended for formal suburban gardens. In the right setting it can be a useful shrub or tree, especially as erosion control along lakes or streams. The handsome toothed leaves appear to be scalloped along the edges. This plant has an open, somewhat rangy growth habit with dark bark.

Carolina Allspice (*Calycanthus floridus*), hardy in Zones 4–9, will grow 6–10 feet tall. The unique brownish-red flowers appear in early spring. They have a spicy smell, but some specimens smell better than others, so choose your favorite at the nursery when in bloom and then plant it near a sitting area or entry to appreciate the lovely fragrance. This plant develops interesting brownish cup-like seedpods that persist throughout the winter. Bog Birch and Carolina Allspice are both deer resistant.

And what about evergreen Shrubs?

Every garden benefits from winter interest, and evergreens do that best. Native species include Arborvitae, Hemlock, Pine, and Spruce. These become huge landscape specimens, unsuitable for most gardens. In the past few years, many dwarf and miniature evergreen shrub cultivars have been introduced. Most grow only ¼-inch to 6 inches per year, so in a 10-year period they will still be small. Some maintain a natural globe shape without excessive pruning. Some are upright. Some are spreaders. As you plan your garden, consider incorporating a few of these little gems into your landscape. They are effective foundation choices or can simply be used as specimen plants. Given their various sizes and shapes, conifers can provide "punctuation" for your garden.

If you find a suitable cultivar at the garden center, check the tag carefully to be sure the mature growth is what you expect. This should tell the mature height in 10 years. The only cultivars considered below are Miniature (M) or Dwarf (D). According to new American Conifer Society guidelines, a Miniature should grow only 3 inches a year, maturing at 2–3 feet. A Dwarf can add 3–6 inches per year, but will still mature at only 3–6 feet. Intermediate and large conifers, like the shade trees in chapter 3, need a large space.

Here, to get you started, are descriptions of a few choices available within each of the four species. Read these descriptions, and then search the Internet for further information. Check out the large wholesale evergreen nurseries such as Iseli Nursery or Stanley and Sons, both located in Oregon. Even though they sell to wholesale buyers exclusively, they provide extensive information on their respective websites. Other nurseries such as Rich's Fox Valley Farm or Greer Garden also have informative websites and generally list hardiness zone, mature size, and predicted annual growth.

American Arborvitae (*Thuja occidentalis*)

'Little Giant' globe
Zones 3–8
1–2 feet

If you enjoy small round shrubs but don't like to prune, this is the choice for you. 'Little Giant' maintains a dense globe shape. It grows very slowly and can eventually reach 4 feet tall and wide. But who knows? You may move before it gets to that size.

Plant it as an accent in the garden or put one on either side of your front door. This shrub will never overgrow its planting space. Give it protection from harsh winds and neighborhood deer and rabbits. Milorganite works as well or better than pricier deer and rabbit repellants, and fertilizes the plants at the same time, so add it to your shopping list.

'Tiny Tim'
Zones 2–8
8–20 inches
Imagine having such a tiny evergreen. It only grows about 15 inches in 10 years. It has the delicate fan-shaped Arborvitae foliage, and as the season progresses to winter the bright green changes to bronze for a nice wintery accent. Nursery sources report it is smaller and more compact than 'Hetz Midget.' It is not fussy about growing conditions. Everything you will read about 'Tiny Tim' is positive. Another oval shaped tiny tot is 'Teddy', who grows to 9–18 inches. These are really cute little specimens and such fun to grow.

Canadian Hemlock (*Tsuga canadensis*)

'Jervis'
Zones 4–8
1–3 feet tall
'Jervis' is one of the smallest hemlock cultivars, remaining tiny for years. Crowded, irregularly spaced branches reach rigidly upward, as if in supplication. The short, medium to dark green needles are densely packed together, and fat new buds fan outward like crests.

This slow-growing pyramidal upright increases only 1–3 inches per year. Eventually it can become 2 feet tall and a little wider. Similar in form to 'Hussi', 'Jervis' is a little more compact and not quite as open.

'Jeddeloh'

Zones 3–7

1–3 feet tall

Gardeners in Germany have appreciated this little conifer for many years. J. D. zu Jeddeloh reportedly found the original seedling of 'Jeddeloh' growing in a cemetery shortly after World War II and introduced it in 1950.

A slow-growing, spreading mound, its branches spiral out from the center and create a nest-like depression in the center of the plant. Its beautiful bright green foliage is backed with pale green.

Provide humus-rich, well-drained, neutral to slightly acidic soil. It will not tolerate alkaline soil, nor does it like drought. It needs its own space and refuses to compete with nearby aggressive roots.

Eastern White Pine (*Pinus strobus*)

'Beran'

Zones 3–6

2 feet

'Beran', another globe-shaped dwarf conifer, makes a mounded little bun. It has a blue gray color, is easy to grow, does not get windburn, and is not fussy about the planting site. It has the typical long needled form, and the dark brown candles create an interesting color contrast to the blue-green needles. It is a handsome little guy and can be tucked into a corner, grown as a foundation plant, or used as a specimen in the garden.

'Blue Shag'

Zones 3–8

2–4 feet

'Blue Shag' resembles a tiny Mugo pine, but gardeners know Mugos are from Japan. This is native all over the eastern United States. It has an intense blue cast to the 5-bundled needles and, as it matures, will produce interesting cones.

Provide rich, well-drained, slightly acidic soil. It cannot tolerate alkaline soil or poor drainage. Like its big brother, 'Blue Shag' will develop brown needles that shed, but anyone who grows white pine knows that is normal behavior and nothing to worry about.

Jackpine (*Pinus banksiana*)

'Angel'
Zones 2–7
3–4 feet
Another pine species with miniature and dwarf introductions is Jackpine. I live on Jackpine Trail and have always wished I could plant that evergreen on our property, but these full-sized trees are far too large. I was delighted to find little 'Angel'. Its tiny bright green needles are less than 1/2 inch in length and it generally does not exceed 4 feet. Jackpine typically twists and turns itself into semi-contorted shapes and this little conical dwarf selection is no different. The interesting shape and the small size will intrigue visitors to your garden. It is part of the Jerry Morris Rocky Mountain collection. I must find a spot for one!

Spruce (*Picea glauca*)

Dwarf Alberta Spruce
Zones 2–8
5–10 feet
Dwarf Alberta Spruce is available at most garden centers. I am including it in this section not because I recommend it nor because it is as small or slow growing as some of the other choices, but because I thought my experience might be helpful.

I planted a Dwarf Alberta Spruce "forest" behind the house as part of a foundation planting thinking it would remain petite. Unfortunately my forest grew larger and faster than I anticipated. I am not good about pruning regularly and try to choose plants accordingly. Now I am faced with a dilemma. "To prune, or not to prune, that is the question." I may have to put up with larger trees than I want or remove my forest and find another slower-growing dwarf.

One other common problem of Dwarf Alberta Spruce is winter burn, especially in northern climates. I know from experience that you can prune off the browned needles in spring and this evergreen will rejuvenate, but sometimes it is necessary to remove so much growth that the tree becomes misshapen and ugly. The sales representative at Iseli Nursery told me it's best to plant these evergreens on the north side of the house or where trees can protect them in winter. Because the summer sun is at a higher angle, Alberta

Spruce can grow in full sun with no ill effects and do not need to be sited close to a building.

He suggested trying *Picea glauca* 'Echiniformis' as an alternative. Here is the information on this selection.

'Echiniformis'
Zones 3–6
1–2 feet
A common name for this dwarf white spruce is "Hedgehog," and when you see it, you can appreciate the nickname. It is a bristly-looking shrub that grows wider than tall and eventually looks like an uncomfortable little cushion. But then you would not sit on a hedgehog either.

It has bluish-gray needles and is relatively carefree. Gardeners often incorporate 'Echiniformis' into rock gardens and if the specimen they purchase is particularly tiny, it makes a nice addition to a trough garden or planter. It can also be planted in a regular perennial garden, or near the front door to elicit comments.

Blue Nest Spruce (*Picea mariana*)

'Nana'
Zones 4–7
6–18 inches
Deer resistant
This familiar shrub has strong blue-green coloring. It is often used as part of a foundation planting, near the driveway or front walk, or as a specimen plant. It also makes a good property line planting. It can be used as a ground cover in part of the garden and will split as it grows and clambers over rocks. It has small needles that are less than 1/2 inch long. This dwarf grows only about 1 inch per year.

The American Conifer Society has an extensive website as do many nurseries that specialize in these evergreen beauties. In addition to the species listed, look at Juniper and Chamaecyparis and see what miniature and dwarf selections might be available in your zone.

As you plan your garden, put dwarf conifers on your want list. These little punctuation marks deserve attention and will definitely make your yard zing.

More than anything I must have flowers, always, always.
—Claude Monet, French painter

5.
Prolific
Perennials

Flowers, Flowers,

Flowers!

Native-plant enthusiasts call them forbs. Plant nurseries and garden centers identify them as perennials. Gardeners refer to them simply as flowers. Whatever you call them, these are the plants that light up the garden, bringing color, fragrance, and beauty to the landscape and earning compliments from passersby.

Gardeners are often surprised to learn how many familiar, gardenworthy plants are native. Coreopsis and Black-eyed Susan have been perennial garden anchors for decades. Recently, gardeners have become excited about the huge flowers of perennial hibiscus that bloom in late summer. Do you grow asters? Or sedum? Or spiderwort? All these familiar plants are native. Let us take time to describe some of them and to add a few more to our repertoire.

Prairie plants are usually what people envision when they hear "native plant." Unfortunately, their reputation for being weedy is well earned. Many gardeners who yearn to fill their sunny front yards with waving grasses and beautiful flowers believe that if you remove the grass, sprinkle a few seeds on the existing soil, and dampen the ground,

Purple Prairie Clover

nature will do the rest. That is not the case. Rather, the result is an unkempt, terrible looking yard and the natives get a bad rap.

Savvy gardeners understand that a native perennial garden takes just as much time, care, and patience to establish as a rose or hosta garden. The main difference is that once a native plant garden is established, it is much less labor intensive. It will not demand all the tasks necessary to maintain that "perfect" rose or hosta garden. With proper planning, a garden with native perennials is just as pretty as one with plants from Europe or Asia, and there are even bonuses. Gardens incorporating natives help restore part of the natural habitat that is lost when we build a house and plant turf grass around it. Each area of the United States has its own specific beauty that we can emulate in our gardens by using the plants of the area. Why choose plants from England or Japan if you live in Indiana or Missouri? Besides, maintenance will be minimized and you will spend less money on chemicals and fertilizer. Best of all, your yard will attract more butterflies. Guaranteed!

I told you I was passionate about gardening. As a native-plant enthusiast, I love spreading the word about the value of using native plants in home landscapes. It is so exciting to discover those first spring wildflowers blooming where yesterday there were none.

I try to have something blooming in my gardens throughout the entire growing season beginning with the earliest spring bulbs that push up through the snow. I love the prairie flowers that laugh at the heat of summer. I appreciate the quiet loveliness of autumn beauties that continue blooming even as temperatures plummet and tumbling leaves create a carpet of gold. I plant native species whenever I can but, as I confessed earlier in this book, I unapologetically include many of their cultivars in my gardens too. Each gardener must make that decision alone. If you are a purist, stick with the native species. If the goal is to restore a woodland, wetland, or native prairie, by all means choose the native species exclusively, and avoid the cultivars. But if you want a pretty flower garden in your home landscape and would rather use native plants or their hybridized offspring instead of planting exotic plants that originate across the sea, then make no apologies and do not feel guilty. It is OK. Go ahead and visit the native-plant-cultivar "candy store" and have fun.

This chapter presents descriptions of approximately100 native perennials that will thrive in the home garden organized by bloom time: spring, summer, or fall. Under individual plant descriptions within each season, I note whether the bloom time is early spring (March/April), spring (March–May), late spring (April–May), summer (June–August), or fall (September–October). But seasons come and go as they will. In a warm year a summer bloomer may begin blooming in May. Obviously, warmer zones will enjoy earlier blooming times than their northern counterparts. Bloom time is not hard and fast, but will give you a general idea of when to expect a particular plant to flower.

Within each season, I arrange perennials by size—small to large—reasoning that most gardeners want their flower gardens, native or not, to be arranged in an orderly manner. It is not uncommon to plant the little guys at the front, medium-sized plants throughout the majority of the garden, and those really tall basses at the back of the choir. You may prefer mixing it up, but the descriptions will identify "who is taller than whom."

I hope this organization will help the average urban or suburban homeowner plan a garden that will bloom throughout the growing season.

Suggested Flowers

SPRING

Short: Front of the Garden

Pasque Flower (*Pulsatilla patens*, aka *Anemone patens*)
Zones 3–8
4–12 inches
Blooms: Very early spring
Lavender flowers
Native to United States and northern Eurasia
Pasque Flower is also known as Prairie Crocus because it resembles our common garden crocus except that the flower is larger. Blooms appear in early spring when it is 4–5 inches tall, before the foliage is fully open. The color is usually lavender to violet with bright yellow centers. It can also be white.

Other names include Easter Crocus (indicative of its blooming time) and Wind Flower. In addition to its many common names, Pasque Flower has a multitude of botanical names. You can usually locate it under one of the preferred names listed above.

After the flower fades, the foliage grows taller. The seeds, on wispy tendrils, spout out like a puff of delicate smoke, somewhat reminiscent of a dandelion. Pasque Flower's leaves are finely cut, like those of a buttercup. After blooming, the foliage can be cut to the ground and will resprout into a tidy clump.

Hummingbirds and butterflies are attracted to the nectar and bees to the early pollen. Pasque Flower (*P. hirsutissima*) was named the state flower of South Dakota in 1903.

PLANTING REQUIREMENTS
The only real requirement for this early spring beauty is good drainage. It will grow in full sun or light shade. Average soil is acceptable. If it becomes too dry, Pasque Flower may go dormant early, but never fear—it will reemerge next spring.

PROPAGATION
Divide established plants immediately after flowering or in the fall. This plant grows from a taproot, so it can also be propagated by root cuttings in early spring or late fall, or by planting seed in the fall. (I have not had much luck with seeds.)

Bird's-Foot Violet (*Viola pedata*)
Zones 4–9
3–6 inches
Blooms: Spring
Dark purple to lavender flowers
Deer resistant
Rain garden
Rock garden
Even though this particular violet is more difficult to establish than common blue violets, it's worth the effort if you are a butterfly lover. It attracts several butterflies and skippers and is the larval food source of the Regal Fritillary butterfly. It also provides nectar for hummingbirds and bees. Pretty little lavender to purple flowers look upward from delicately lobed palmate foliage thought to resemble a bird's foot—hence the common name.

Locate this pretty plant along the path where it can be appreciated as you stroll through the garden in early spring. It is a nice addition to a rock wall.

PLANTING REQUIREMENTS

Bird's-Foot Violet requires well-drained, dry to medium moist soil in full sun or part shade. It is drought tolerant and does not appreciate wet feet. In fact, continuous moisture signals a sure death.

PROPAGATION

Like many violets, the Bird's-Foot Violet has capsular seedpods that explode, sending copper-colored seeds scattering hither and yon. The seeds are coated with a sticky, sweet residue that attracts ants, which carry them off to their nests, helping to distribute them.

Prairie Smoke (*Geum triflorum*)

Zones 3–7

6–12 Inches

Blooms: Late spring to early summer

Dark purple, pink, to rosy red flowers

Rain garden

Rock garden

Some people identify Prairie Smoke as Purple Avens. Whatever you call it, this is a cool plant. And it likes its temperatures cool at bedtime too. Delicate, rosy red, bud-like flowers emerge in very early spring. When the seeds begin to ripen, hairy plumes resembling wisps of rosy-mauve smoke push out from the faded flowers. Some describe the seed plumes as whiskers, giving rise to another common name, Old Man's Beard. A mass of Prairie Smoke looks just like the name, hovering above the ground. Prairie Smoke can be used as a ground cover.

PLANTING REQUIREMENTS

Prairie Smoke prefers full sun and a dry planting site. Even though this plant can thrive in a moist planting site, it cannot tolerate wet feet, especially in winter, so be sure the soil is well drained. It enjoys afternoon shade in extremely hot sites. It is recommended for the drier edges of a rain garden and for a rock garden

PROPAGATION

After the seeds have ripened, the leaves continue to grow, sometimes stretching to 16 inches. Plant ripened seeds or transplant young plants.

Keep the soil moist until the new plants are established. Prairie Smoke grows from ground-hugging rosettes that often stay evergreen throughout the winter.

Marsh Marigold (*Caltha palustris* L.)

Zones 2–8

12–18 inches

Blooms: Early spring

Yellow flowers

Sun/part shade

Deer resistant

Native to United States, Europe, Asia

Marsh Marigold prefers growing in a marsh, but will perform faithfully in loamy garden soil as long as it is reasonably moist. My plant grows near a downspout and blooms profusely each spring with beautiful, shiny, bright yellow, buttercup-like blossoms at a time when any hint of color is welcomed. Large, heart-shaped leaves grow even larger after flowering ends. When summer temperatures rise too high, Marsh Marigold simply goes dormant, then awakens the following spring.

Caltha palustris var. 'Flore Pleno' has large, yellow, double blooms.and reaches a height of 12 inches. *Caltha palustris* var. 'Alba' (white) is a compact form that blooms a little earlier than the species and is smaller (6–9 inches tall). Single flowers are white.

Beware of an invasive, exotic lookalike and avoid it at all costs. Lesser Celandine (*Ranunculus ficaria*) from Eurasia is an inveterate invader and will take over wildflower areas, lawns, and anywhere else it can get its nutlets situated. It has a seductive, shiny, buttercup-like flower and scalloped leaves. It blooms about a month after Marsh Marigold. I was delighted when an Indianapolis neighbor gave me a good-sized start. Before long it was everywhere. I dug it out repeatedly, only to have it come roaring back in triplicate the following spring. It is an ephemeral, but when it dies back it leaves a solid mat of leaf debris that dares anything to penetrate it. Consequently everything around and below it dies and soon there is nothing except shiny yellow flowers followed by a desert of dead foliage. So be wary of pass-along so-called Marsh Marigolds even if they come from reliable garden-club friends.

PLANTING REQUIREMENTS

My Marsh Marigold thrives in a naturally damp spot in the back yard. It prefers loamy garden soil kept reasonably moist, especially in spring during blooming, but tolerates drier soil once it goes dormant. It does best in full sunlight.

PROPAGATION

Increase your stock by dividing established clumps immediately after blooming. Keep well watered after dividing. Seeds will germinate, but take up to three years to bloom. Marsh Marigold is available from native-plant mail-order nurseries.

Golden Alexanders (*Zizia aurea*)

Zones 3–8

12–24 inches

Blooms: Late spring

Yellow flowers

Sun/part sun

Golden umbels cover this airy green plant in late spring. The flower heads remind me of dill and after the gold of the flowers disappears the remaining brownish seed heads look even more like dill. This plant is a member of the carrot family, so watch for striking Black Swallowtail caterpillars munching on the leaves. Soon there will be gorgeous Black Swallowtail butterflies flitting about the yard. I usually plant carrot seeds as well as edible parsley near my Golden Alexanders to encourage Swallowtails to keep coming back. They love anything in the carrot and parsley family.

The heart-shaped, serrated-edged foliage of Heart-Leaved Golden Alexanders (Z. *aptera*) is handsome even after the flowers have completed their blooms, which makes this plant another all-season standout in the garden.

PLANTING REQUIREMENTS

Golden Alexanders flourish in average, moist soil and can also tolerate periods of dryness as long as the soil is well drained. Plant this handsome plant near the front of the garden and provide as much sun as possible for best results.

Divide the fibrous rooted plants or transplant young seedlings. Planting seed can work but be advised that it isn't always successful. Division might be easier.

Spiderwort (*Tradescantia virginiana* L.)
Zones 4–9
15–24 inches
Blooms: Spring to early summer
Blue, white, or pink flowers
Full sun/light shade
Deer resistant
Rain garden

Spiderwort flowers have three petals. These bloom above long, thin, green leaves in late spring or early summer, opening in early morning and closing by late afternoon. As with daylilies, each flower lasts only a single day, but there are so many buds it doesn't matter. Cut the foliage to the ground after blooming. New foliage will resprout in a tidy clump of green and the plant will bloom again in late summer.

Butterflies and hummingbirds enjoy the nectar. Multiple colors are available in the nursery trade including white 'Osprey' with airy, purple stamens; large-flowered white 'Innocence'; and hot pink 'Red Cloud'. Ohio Spiderwort (*T. ohiensis*) is a similar plant. Check the nursery when plants are in bloom to choose your favorite.

PLANTING REQUIREMENTS
Average garden soil with adequate moisture and good drainage will satisfy this plant as long as there is ample sunlight. Spiderwort loves full sun. It will flop and not bloom as well in too much shade. This is one plant that will survive under a Black Walnut tree.

PROPAGATION
Divide in spring or fall. Reseeds freely.

Medium: Middle of the Garden

Wild Hyacinth (*Camassia* spp.)
Zones 3–9

2–4 feet

Blooms: Spring

Blue flowers

Long, wide, strappy green leaves emerge from the Camas bulb early in spring. Star-like blue flowers float high above the leaves, surprising me each spring when they suddenly appear. Like any spring bulb, it blooms and then takes in nourishment for the following year through its leaves. The leaves yellow and die to the ground, so mark the spot to keep from accidentally digging it up. It is worth protecting.

Native Camas species include *C. leichtlinii, C. quamash, and C. cusickii.* Several hybrids and cultivars are available in the nursery trade. Look for 'Blue Danube' with deep purple flowers; 'Zwanenburg', a true blue; *C. leichtlinii* 'Caerulea', with soft lavender-blue flowers; or *C. leichtlinii* 'Alba', a bluish-white. The large, creamy, white flowers of 'Semiplena' are double. But I like the delicate blue flowers of *C. scilloides* best of all.

One of the most tragic episodes in U.S. history involves the Camas plant (previously spelled "Kamas"). From time immemorial, Shoshone and Bannock Indians harvested Camas bulbs, their vegetable food staple, on a lush prairie in what is now Camas County, Idaho. Treaty negotiations in 1868 designated this prairie as reservation land for these people. But when written up and ratified, the treaty assigned "Kansas Prairie" to them. Whether this occurred by accident or design is still disputed. What is not disputed is that, to date, these tribes have not received the promised prairie where nutritious Camas plants once waved their blue blossoms. Nor have they received "Kansas Prairie." Nobody knows where the latter might be.

PLANTING REQUIREMENTS

Plant the bulbs 5–8 inches deep, depending on their size, in loamy, well-drained soil in the fall. Provide moisture during the growing season. It is drought tolerant later in the season after the plant goes dormant.

PROPAGATION

The easiest way to start is to purchase bulbs from a mail-order catalog. Camassia forms clumps as daffodils do, which increase in size over the years. Separate bulbils from the mother bulb after the flowers fade and the leaves turn yellow, or mark the spot to dig and separate after the plant goes dormant. Camassia has small seed capsules that hold shiny little black seeds. The plants will self-sow in moist soil, but new seedlings take four years to flower. Seeds need moist cold stratification to germinate.

Wild Geranium (*Geranium maculatum*)
Zones 3–9
15–24 inches
Blooms: Late spring
Lavender-pink flowers
Sun/part shade
Rain garden

Wild Geranium, more commonly used in woodland gardens, will accept full sun as long as the planting site is kept reasonably moist during the heat of summer. It is covered with small lavender-pink flowers in early spring. Wild Geranium retains its compact, tidy shape after blooming so it makes a nice green center-of-the-garden perennial after its early spring flower display. The interesting leaves are palmate, cut nearly to the base, like 5–7 fat fingers. If the soil gets too dry, the leaves will turn yellow and the plant will simply go dormant until the following spring.

 G. bicknellii has smaller, pale rose flowers. *G. richardsonii* blooms in the summer and has white flowers.

PLANTING REQUIREMENTS
Give it rich, loamy, moist soil, and keep it well watered during periods of drought.

PROPAGATION
Self-sows. Transplanting mature specimens in spring is seldom successful. Wait until fall to divide the coarse, brittle rhizome after the plant goes dormant.

Wild Columbine (*Aquilegia canadensis*)
Zones 3–9
12–30 inches
Blooms: Late spring
Red-and-yellow flowers
Full sun/part shade
Deer and rabbit resistant
Rain garden

Wild Columbine is a no-brainer for the perennial border, blooming happily for several weeks. Drooping, red-and-yellow flowers float on wiry stems above the pretty foliage. Once the seedpods have dried, cut the entire plant to the ground. New leaves will resprout and remain as a tidy clump for the rest of the season.

Columbine flowers are a favorite nectar source of hummingbirds and the leaves are a larval food for the Columbine Duskywing butterfly. Leaf miners run willy-nilly through the leaves, but the only problem they cause is cosmetic, so ignore their white trails.

There are many hybrids of the native wildflower. McKenna Hybrids boast a wide variety of colors, shapes, and sizes, even some that are double. Dwarf varieties are particularly effective at the front of a border. Check your local nursery when plants are in bloom to choose your favorite.

Rocky Mountain Columbine (*A. caerulea*), the state flower of Colorado, has a lovely blue and white flower. A red variation is called 'Rotstern'. These self-sow readily.

PLANTING REQUIREMENTS
Grows well in average, well-drained soil in full sun or part shade.

PROPAGATION
Mature plants resent changing spots, so increase your stock by seeding or moving young plants. Young seedlings can be moved successfully as long as they are kept well watered until established. Collect dried seedpods and shake the tiny black seeds wherever you want new plants to grow, or save them in a paper bag. Stratify saved seeds in the humidrawer of the refrigerator and sprinkle them on top of moist, bare soil in 2–4 weeks or in the fall. Do not cover. The rain will work them into the soil.

Prairie Phlox (*Phlox pilosa* var. *ozarkana*)
Zones 4–9
12–24 Inches
Blooms: Late spring
Rosy-lavender or violet flowers
Beautiful deep rosy-lavender flowers blanket this low-growing phlox in late spring. The flowers face upward, so this is a favorite of butterflies and

hummingbirds. "Pilosa" means hairy, one of its distinguishing characteristics. Prairie Phlox will spread.

PLANTING REQUIREMENTS
Average soil. Will tolerate moist or dry conditions as long as the site is well drained.

PROPAGATION
Spreads by underground runners. Take stem cuttings in spring or root cuttings in the fall.

Blue Star Amsonia (*Amsonia tabernaemontana* 'Montana')
Zones 4–9
12–18 inches
Blooms: Late spring
Blue flowers
Sun/part shade
Deer resistant
Rain garden

Beautiful star-like, sky-blue flowers appear on this airy plant in late spring and early summer. The tiny flowers on my Amsonia plant have always been pure white, but I have never seen a duplicate. Amsonia grows into an airy, feathery bush, making a nice statement in the garden long after the fragrant blossoms disappear. In the fall, the willow-like leaves become clear yellow.

The species, hardy in Zones 3–9, grows to 36 inches. The flowers are more intense blue than 'Montana' and blooming begins a couple weeks earlier.

Cultivars: 'Blue Ice' is a very compact, heavy-blooming plant with dark blue flowers. 'Short Stack', introduced by Plant Delights Nursery in North Carolina, generally matures at only 10 inches. It is reputedly hardy in Zones 5–9, but the jury is still out on hardiness farther north. Give it a try!

Hubricht's Amsonia (*A. hubrichtii*) is hardy in Zones 5–8. A Missouri Botanical Garden Plant of Merit, its leaves are much finer and more needle-like than those of *A. tabernaemontana*, changing to bright golden yellow in the fall. Deer resistant, it grows 12–36 inches tall. Blue flowers bloom in late spring. This particular Amsonia does fine in either sun or part shade. It is similar to Fringed Bluestar (*A. ciliata*). Planting requirements and propagation echo those of Blue Star Amsonia (*A. tabernaemontana*) below.

PLANTING REQUIREMENTS
Amsonia is a very forgiving plant, but results are best with full sun. It is not fussy about soil or moisture as long as the drainage is adequate, and will thrive just about anywhere. It prefers sun and can flop in shady locations.

PROPAGATION
Plant ripened seeds in fall. The seeds resemble milkweed pods. Divide in spring or fall, but once this plant is established it is preferable to leave it undisturbed.

Sundrops (*Oenothera fruticosa*)
Zones 3–8
12–24 inches
Blooms: Late spring
Yellow flowers
Drought tolerant
Deer resistant
I call Sundrops "Kath's Plant" because I got my original plant from my younger sister Kathryn, who died of breast cancer when she was only 43. Sundrops, like my sister, are bright and happy and never fail to make me smile when they bloom. The reddish buds open to color-crayon-yellow and grow from ground-hugging rosettes. 'Fyrverkeri' aka 'Fireworks' is a more compact 18-inch form. Missouri Primrose (*O. macrocarpa* aka *O. missouriensis*) has even larger yellow flowers, sometimes as wide as 5 inches across. Its foliage grows close to the ground. Sundrops' nectar attracts butterflies and hummingbirds.

Showy Evening Primrose (*O. speciosa*) is often called Pink Ladies. Despite its soft, pale pink flowers, it can be aggressive, so beware! It might be best planted as a ground cover where it is free to roam at will. Unlike the yellow forms, it may go dormant in extreme drought, resprouting when fall rains return.

This plant is short, seldom exceeding 12–18 inches tall. Its soft pink flowers open in the evening and close in the morning. In southern regions, Pink Ladies can get days and nights mixed up, opening in the morning. Each flower lasts only one day.   A white form called 'Alba' is available, but most cultivars have yellow flowers of varying sizes and hues.

Missouri Evening Primrose (*O. macrocarpa* aka *O. missouriensis*) spreads readily. It is suitable for a rock garden or can be used as a sprawling, floriferous ground cover with lemon-yellow sundrop flowers on low red stems. It can bloom from May to August and prefers a dry planting site.

PLANTING REQUIREMENTS
Plant in average, well-drained garden soil. Full sun is best for heavy flowering.

PROPAGATION
Divide the ground-hugging rosettes in early spring or fall. Will self-sow, but planting seeds is not always successful.

Tall: Back of the Garden

Wild Lupine (*Lupinus perennis* L.)
Zones 3–9
Blooms: Early summer
Blue, pink, white flowers
Sun/part shade
Lupine is the host plant for the endangered Karner Blue butterfly. Other butterflies that utilize this plant during their life cycle include Common Blue, Silvery Blue, Frosted Elfin, and Elf, so consider planting some of the native species even though the flowering may not be as spectacular as the hybrid forms.

Unfortunately, deer consider Lupine a tasty treat and will nibble it to the ground. Warning: seeds can be toxic.

Hybrid Wild Lupine (*Lupinus × hybrida*)

Wild Lupine hybrids are more popular with gardeners and bloom more reliably than the species. A wonderful array of colors is available including the usual blues, whites, and purples, plus shades of pink, red, and even yellow. Tall racemes of pea-like flowers soar above the interesting palmate foliage. These plants are hardy to Zones 4–8. They are usually between 18 and 48 inches tall, depending on the particular plant. Just as does the Wild Lupine, these hybrids bloom in the summer.

For front-of-the-border, 18-inch dwarf varieties look for 'Minarette', which comes in a variety of colors. Or check out the Popsicle or Gallery offerings.

PLANTING REQUIREMENTS

Lupine thrives in average well-drained soil and is drought tolerant. It does not tolerate wet feet, and in too much moisture the deep taproot will rot. A legume, Lupine fixes nitrogen in the soil.

PROPAGATION

The seed capsules explode, so this plant self-sows readily. Plant ripened seeds immediately, otherwise you will need an inoculum to get them to germinate properly. It has a very long, deep taproot and does not transplant well. If the garden site has never had Lupines, the seeds will require an inoculum to germinate. Most seed nurseries provide this without charge.

For hybrids, gardeners must either purchase the hybrid seed or potted plants since self-sown hybrid seeds never breed true.

Blue Flag Iris (*Iris virginica* var. *shrevei*)
Wild Iris (*Iris versicolor*)

Zones 2–8
18–36 inches
Blooms: Late spring to early summer
Lavender-blue or purple flowers
Rain garden
Blue Flag Iris blooms during May and early June, followed by Wild Iris in June and July, so if you alternate a mass of both species there will be irises blooming

for quite a while. Unlike common garden iris, these species do not have the familiar beard.

Attracts butterflies and hummingbirds.

PLANTING REQUIREMENTS

Usually grown in a bog or wet garden, these iris species will also thrive in any continually moist planting area. They cannot tolerate drought. Good choice for a rain garden.

PROPAGATION

Divide the large rhizome clumps in midsummer right after blooming and replant immediately so the plants become established early in the season.

Beardtongue (*Penstemon digitalis*)

Zones 3–8

18–48 inches

Blooms: Spring to early summer

White flowers

Sun/part shade

Drought tolerant

Deer and rabbit resistant

Penstemon forms clumps and can stretch 4–5 feet tall if it is happy. Hummingbirds love the tubular flowers. It also attracts butterflies. 'Husker Red' was named for its reddish foliage, pink flowers, and red buds. The new, improved variety called 'Dark Towers', with darker, glossy red-bronze foliage and light pink flowers, is even more striking. Both mature at about 30 inches tall.

For a smaller Penstemon, try Southwestern Penstemon (*P. barbatus*) especially the cultivar 'Jingle Bells' with bright orange-red flowers. It grows 18–24 inches tall. 'Elfin Pink'— the smallest cultivar, at 12 inches— has rose pink flowers and will rebloom if cut back.

PLANTING REQUIREMENTS

Average, well-drained soil. Does fine in wet or dry conditions. Penstemon is less apt to flop and blooms better in full sun, but will survive in a partly shaded spot.

PROPAGATION
Plant seeds in fall or divide mature plants in spring or fall.

Purple Meadow Rue (*Thalictrum dasycarpum*)
Zones 3–8
3–5 feet
Blooms: Late spring to early summer
White or dusty lavender-rose flowers
Full sun/part shade
Deer resistant

Sturdy purple stalks hold the fluffy flowers of Purple Meadow Rue, also known as Tall Meadow Rue. This tall, airy plant dislikes extreme heat so southern gardeners may need to provide additional moisture during hot and humid weather.

Early Meadow Rue (*T. dioicum*) grows in similar moist conditions, also blooming in early spring, but this species is considerably smaller, maturing at 24 inches. It is dioecious with both male (yellow stamens) and female (purple pistil) plants. It has greenish-white flowers and pretty, columbine-like leaves.

PLANTING REQUIREMENTS
Average, well-drained soil that is reasonably moist. Does not tolerate drought.

PROPAGATION
Seeds ripen and turn dark in the fall. Plant immediately or cold stratify for later planting. Transplant small self-sown seedlings in spring or fall, keeping them well watered until established.

Blue False Indigo (*Baptisia australis*)
Zones 3–9
30–48 inches
Blooms: Late spring to early summer
Blue flowers
Full sun/partial shade

Drought tolerant

Deer resistant

Rain garden

Baptisia becomes a tall, bushy shrub with blue-green foliage that is perfect for the back of the garden. In late spring and early summer its profuse, lupine-like racemes of intense blue flowers open from bottom to top. Dark capsular seedpods distinguish this plant in the fall, creating unmistakable sounds as they shiver in the wind. Indigo refers to the blue of the flowers, used by pioneers and Native Americans to dye cloth. It is called "false" because the color is not as intense as the true indigos that come from the West Indies. If white flowers are your thing, then grow Wild White Indigo (*B. alba*). It literally glows in the landscape, even at dusk.

A number of colors and sizes have been hybridized. *Baptisia* × 'Purple Smoke', introduced by the North Carolina Botanical Garden, has "purple-eyed, smoky-purple flowers." For fantastic spires of brilliant yellow, you can't go wrong with 'Screaming Yellow' (*B. sphaerocarpa*). It blooms heavily and matures at about 3 feet. A hybrid of *B. alba* × *B. sphaerocarpa* resulted in 'Carolina Moonlight'. The delicate, buttery yellow flowers will light up the spring garden.

Recent commercial releases from the plant breeding program at the Chicago Botanical Garden include 'Solar Flare Prairieblues', a yellow-flowered version that matures at 24–30 inches. These flowers change from lemon-yellow to rich orange; the contrast between the bottom and top of each raceme is a real showstopper. Look for the reblooming, 4-foot, vase-shaped 'Midnight Prairieblues' with extra large blue-violet flowers or the smaller 3-foot 'Twilite Prairieblues', with deep violet flowers. In fact, check out all their offerings for some really fantastic new plants.

Baptisia deserves to be a focal point in your garden. Just do not try to move it once you decide where to plant it!

PLANTING REQUIREMENTS

For the best flowers and the strongest stems, grow this bushy plant in well-drained, average soil in full sun. Granted, it will take partial shade, but for the best show, choose full sun. It likes ample moisture, but once established it is very drought tolerant.

PROPAGATION

Mature plants have extremely deep, massive root systems so division is not an option. Transplant young seedlings or soak the mature seeds overnight and plant in the fall. Up to three years are required for the plant to bloom from seed. For faster results, just choose a color and buy it!

White Goatsbeard (*Aruncus dioicus*)

Zones 3–8
36–60 inches
Blooms: Late spring to early summer
White flowers
Full sun/partial shade
Native to United States, Europe, and Asia
Rain garden

Goatsbeard is guaranteed to elicit a "What is that?" from garden visitors. It resembles a giant Astilbe with huge, feathery plumes of creamy white above dark green, long-lasting foliage. This noninvasive, clump-forming perennial makes a bold statement at the back of any border. After the flowers finish blooming, gardeners have two options. They can leave the flowers to dry or cut the stalks back to create a tidy clump of green for the remainder of the growing season. I usually let my flowers remain on the plant even into the winter, but I also do that with Astilbe because I like that tan architectural touch the dried flower heads provide.

Aruncus is a nectar source for hummingbirds and butterflies and the larval food host for the Dusky Azure butterfly.

PLANTING REQUIREMENTS
Goatsbeard prefers rich, loamy soil, but will grow in average soil and will even accept occasional dryness. To grow in full sun, provide plenty of moisture or the leaves will brown along the edges. In hot, humid areas, provide adequate moisture and partial shade.

PROPAGATION
Divide in spring or fall or plant ripened seed in fall.

SUMMER

Short: Front of the Garden

Nodding Wild Onion (*Allium cernuum*)
Zones 3–9
8–18 inches
Blooms: Early summer
Rose, pale pink, or white flowers
Sun/partial sun
Drought tolerant
Deer resistant
The foliage is reminiscent of small green onions in the produce department and grows from a single point in the ground. The flower stalk soars up from the center holding a large flower umbel. The large "lollipop" umbels nod, so only bees are brave enough to hang upside down to gather nectar.

A late-blooming beauty named 'Leo' can reach up to 30 inches. Dense clusters of white flowers open in August, extending the normal bloom season. 'Oxy White' (aka *A. oxyphilum*) is a delicate version with airy, bright white flowers.

PLANTING REQUIREMENTS
Plant in well-drained, average garden soil in full or partial sun. Gardeners in extremely hot zones may want to provide afternoon shade, but these bloom best in full sun.

PROPAGATION
Plant the tiny, shiny, black seeds after they ripen or dig and divide the red, onion-like bulbs in fall. The plants form larger clumps as they age, like daffodils, and can self-sow if conditions are good. They are not invasive.

Monkey Flower (*Mimulus ringens*)
Zones 2–9
12–30 inches
Blooms: Summer
Lavender-pink or blue-violet flowers

(*Above*) The author's newly planted garden in-corporates three pots of annuals on standards to provide season-long color. A rain barrel collects roof run-off for watering. (*Lower left*) The author solved a roof drainage dilemma by directing a PVC pipe under the new sidewalk installation to a pop-up drain in a rain garden. (*Lower right*) Bright pink turtlehead provides vertical interest.

(*Above*) A Blue Thumb grant provided funding for a neighborhood rain garden project. A curb cut, incorporated at the edge of the street, is part of the required drainage design.

(*Opposite*) Minnesota's Dakota County Master Gardeners designed a handsome rain garden to collect runoff from a large parking area. The dry stream directs the water flow into the center of the garden.

A Swallowtail caterpillar is easy to identify. The unusual chrysalis can be hard to spot, but eventually the lovely Swallowtail butterfly emerges to mate, lay eggs and begin the amazing cycle again.

(*Clockwise from upper left*) This young family delights in a newly hatched Monarch butterfly. Monarch caterpillars, with distinctive yellow, white, and black stripes, eventually form a beautiful jade chrysalis decorated with gold. The familiar Monarch butterfly emerges from its chrysalis in 9–14 days and will mate within a week.

Orange Butterfly Weed is one of several beautiful native milk-weeds that provide brilliant color in the garden and sweet nectar for butterflies and hummingbirds. Milkweed leaves are the only food eaten by growing Monarch caterpillars. Seeds (*upper left*) are easy to collect in fall and will readily germinate.

(*Above*) Alex beams as the newborn Monarch "Breezy" climbs on his arm. The minute white monarch egg that eventually became "Breezy" began life on a milkweed leaf (*below left*), hatched 4–6 days later as a tiny caterpillar (*below right*), became a veritable "eating machine" and then enclosed itself in a chrysalis to continue the magical metamorphosis that is part of the life cycle of every Monarch butterfly. *Photo of Alex and Breezy by Tiffany Harstad.*

Native yellow coreopsis brightens
a suburban entry garden.

(*Above*) Native plants spill over a rock wall used as a design element in front of this lovely home. (*Below*) A kidney shaped garden, planted as a colorful living collage, incorporates a variety of native plants that will bloom in succession all season long, beginning early in spring.

(*Above left*) 'Mardi Gras', a colorful cultivar of Sneezeweed, zings in any perennial border.

(*Above right*) Native Sneezeweed can become very tall. It appears at the center back of this native plant garden where it attracts nectar loving butterflies and hummingbirds.

(*Below left*) Huge blossoms of Hardy Hibiscus, also called Rose Mallow, create a focal point at the edge of a native plant garden.

(*Opposite*) Massive Joe-pye Weed, an outstanding addition to a wide perennial border or at the back of a garden, takes command of its space.

(*Inset*) Threadleaf Coreopsis blooms near a pensive cherub.

(*Right*) Blue Flag Iris glistens in the garden after a sudden spring storm.
(*Below left*) Raindrops sparkle on the palmate leaf of a pink Lupine.

(*Opposite*) A silhouetted Red-winged Blackbird sings for its mate high atop the fragrant, blooming branches of a roadside native elderberry bush.

(*Above*) Sundrops are a welcome addition to the early season garden; even their tightly closed red buds contribute a bright splash of color.

(*Opposite*) A large Common Milkweed stands sentinel in the author's front garden, offering food and nectar to passing Monarchs and encouraging these butterfly beauties to take up residence.

Tall purple Blazing Star *(Liatris spicata)* boasts individual florets and blooms from the top down.

Michigan Lily can be easily distinguished from Turk's Cap Lily. Michigan Lily's petals bend sharply up and inwards, while Turk's Cap's curving petals reach heavenward as if in supplication, but do not touch in the center. Michigan Lily greeted pioneers traveling across tallgrass prairies.

(*Above*) An upright clump of grass, a dwarf blue evergreen and an interesting boulder create a visual accent at the corner of a brick wall.

(*Opposite*) A colorful garden spills down the hillside at the side of a suburban home. Rocks anchor the edge of the garden as it meets the lawn below.

(*Above*) Brilliant red Cardinal Flower soars high in the garden, offering tasty nectar to passing hummingbirds and butterflies.

(*Opposite*) Attractive green-centered *Rudbeckia hirta* 'Prairie Sun', a 2003 All-America Selection winner, will bloom the first year from seed and once established may self-sow.

(*Above*) Soft, fuzzy flower-balls bloom above the strappy leaves of Nodding Wild Onion.

(*Opposite*) Flagstones and slate edge an attractive waterfall, accented with native grasses and flowering ground cover.

A floriferous clematis will soften the edge of a
stone wall and attract birds and butterflies.

Tall Goatsbeard creates an effective backdrop in
the perennial garden.

(*Opposite*) A variety of plantings march down a hillside, effectively creating a welcome habitat for wildlife and a colorful scene for passersby.

(*Above*) Cutting through a massive expanse of lawn, this creative perennial border provides sparkle to an otherwise humdrum space.

Notice the use of height, color, and texture to create
an interesting hillside filled with contrasts.

A rock wall shores up a steeply sloped garden space filled with white phlox, masses of bright red *Echinacea* Sombrero 'Salsa Red' and Black-eyed Susan.

Black-eyed Susan, hostas, and Purple Coneflower nestle at the base of a handsome spruce and a towering Red Oak.

Children enjoy pinching the snapdragon-like flowers to make a monkey face. Flowers on this short, bushy plant are usually blue-violet, but occasionally a plant will have pretty pink flowers. Pollinated by bees, Monkey Flower is a nectar host for butterflies and the larval host plant of the Common Buckeye and Checkerspot butterflies and the Chalcedony Midget Moth.

Another species, Winged Monkey Flower (*M. alatus*), can bloom for up to two months in summer as long as its roots are kept moist.

PLANTING REQUIREMENTS
Plant in loamy to slightly acidic soil. Monkey Flower demands consistently moist soil and cannot tolerate dryness, even for short periods of time.

PROPAGATION
Separate rhizomes in the fall, or plant seed. It is not invasive.

Blanket Flower (*Gaillardia arstata*)
Zones 3–9
12–24 inches
Blooms: Summer
Red, orange, and yellow flowers
Deer and rabbit resistant
Rain garden
Blanket Flower gets its common name from the brilliant colors woven into Native American blankets. It is a perfect front-of-the-border perennial and if it is content with its environment can "blanket" the ground. Daisy-like flowers in color-crayon tones will brighten up any garden space. This little beauty attracts hummingbirds and butterflies. What more can a gardener ask?

Multiple Gaillardia cultivars are available. 'Arizona Apricot' was a 2011 All-America Selections (AAS) Winner. More subdued than most gaillardias, its large flowers glow in soft tones of apricot and yellow. 'Mesa Yellow' won the award in 2010. Words can scarcely describe the unusual cultivar 'Fanfare'. The deep red center holds ray flowers that are red at the base, but yellow at the tips. And to top it off, there are tiny individual florets at the tip of each flared ray. This cultivar truly deserves a fanfare! 'Arizona Sun' is a tiny 10-inch star with bright red ray flowers ringed with sunny yellow. 'Bijou' is another small one but what it lacks in stature, it makes up for in sizzle. The 1991 AAS Winner 'Red Plume' has brilliant double scarlet red flowers.

PLANTING REQUIREMENTS

Plant in average, well-drained soil in full sun. This plant cannot tolerate wet feet.

PROPAGATION

Gaillardia is easy to propagate from seed, and even most of the new introductions will breed true. Leave the seedheads over winter. The birds will thank you and next spring there will be self-sown seedlings.

Black-eyed Susan (*Rudbeckia* spp.)

Zones 3–9

18–30 inches tall

Blooms: Mid- to late summer

Golden yellow flowers

Drought tolerant

Deer resistant

Rain garden

Black-eyed Susans (*Rudbeckia hirta*) have those familiar golden-yellow, daisy-like flowers with either a black or brown center. Flowers come in various sizes. They may be biennials or short-lived perennials, but self-sow so exuberantly you will never even notice. The National Garden Bureau declared 2008 the "Year of the Rudbeckia." Check out that website for a wide variety of wonderful choices.

The Missouri Botanical Garden website notes that this plant is often referred to as Gloriosa Daisy. A friend gave me a division and the flowers were indeed glorious, blooming for weeks in shades of yellow, red, and bronzy orange. When my Rudbeckias have finished blooming, I leave a few standing for the birds and reseeding and cut the rest to the ground.

Huge flowers cover the cultivar 'Indian Summer', creating a spectacular summer display. Another of my favorites is 'Prairie Sun', a 2003 AAS Winner hardy in Zones 3–8. It's hard to resist this soft yellow flower with a deep golden blush complementing the smooth, green center. The first year I grew it we had a particularly severe winter and it did not survive. I figured, "Annuals die too," and just purchased another. It is doing fine. Evidently it is possible to grow this beauty from seed, so that is next on my agenda.

'Goldsturm' (*R. fulgida*) is 20–30 inches tall. For a really short version of this delightful species, look for 'City Garden', which grows

9–12 inches tall. Another small rudbeckia is 'Blovi' Viette's Little Suzy (12–18 inches). Either works well in the front of the garden. The 24-inch 'Early Bird Gold' is a popular, well-behaved cultivar. Jellito introduced a new improved 'Goldsturm' named 'Little Goldstar' in 2011. This compact 14–16-inch dwarf Rudbeckia is covered with bright flowers nearly all summer. Walters Gardens, Inc., claims it is "destined to become the new industry standard."

I also grow Brown-eyed Susan (*R. triloba*). It has much smaller flowers than either *R. fulgida* or *R. hirta*. Cute little 2-inch blooms cover this bushy perennial for most of the summer. *R. triloba* blooms next to the larger-flowered Black-eyed Susan make an interesting contrast in the mid- to late summer perennial border.

Sweet Coneflower (*R. subtomentosa*), hardy in Zones 4–9, reaches 4–5 feet tall. Bruised leaves leave a hint of licorice on your hands. 'Henry Eilers', which can become 6 feet tall, has very delicate, thin, ray flowers described in a *Fine Gardening* article as "finely quilled." For another really tall Rudbeckia, search for Great Coneflower *(R. maxima)*. It can soar to 7 feet and makes a strong statement at the back of a perennial garden or among tall grasses in a prairie or meadow.

PLANTING REQUIREMENTS
Black-eyed Susan thrives in average, well-drained soil in full sun. These plants will accept part sun, but will not bloom as well and may flop. They are drought tolerant but do not withstand poor drainage.

PROPAGATION
Self-sows readily, or plant the black seeds in spring or fall. Small, ground-hugging rosettes appear the first year, and bloom as full-sized plants the following summer. Some bloom the first fall. Dig and transplant first-year plants wherever you want to start a new "family."

Coreopsis (*Coreopsis* spp.)
Zones 3–8
12–24 inches
Blooms: Summer
Deer and rabbit resistant
Rain garden

Coreopsis boasts a number of species and sizes, so it is a plant for all gardens. The majority bloom in shades of yellow and gold, but there are a few with hints of pink, white, and rose.

Threadleaf Coreopsis (*Coreopsis verticillata*)

This species is also known as Whorled Coreopsis. The smallest cultivar I know is 'Little Sundial'. This compact 6–12 inch beauty has single, golden-yellow flowers with a dark maroon eye. It also works in containers.

'Moonbeam' is one of my favorite front-of-the-garden perennials. Its soft yellow flowers just glow above an open mound of delicate, pale green, threadlike leaves. Sometimes it seems short-lived in my garden, but I just replace it.

'Zagreb' (15–18 inches tall) has a more intensely yellow flower and may be hardier than 'Moonbeam'. I usually chop these plants back in early August to make them rebloom in the fall.

Lance-leaved Coreopsis (*C. lanceolata*) is a taller, more rounded plant that covers itself with long-lasting, bright yellow flowers. This foolproof native is planted behind 'Moonbeam' in my border and grows to about 18 inches.

Large-Flowered or Prairie Coreopsis (*C. grandiflora*) has larger flowers, is short and compact, and blooms early and long. 'Early Sunrise' has semidouble flowers in shades of yellow and gold.

The narrow green leaves of 'Tequilla Sunrise', a hybrid of *C. lanceolata* and *C. grandiflora*, are edged in yellow and cream. Introduced by Ken and Linda Smith of Columbus, Ohio, it is hardy in Zones 5–10. The flowers are deep gold with a maroon eye-ring.

Pink Tickseed (*C. rosea*) matures at 12–24 inches tall. The species has soft pink flowers and has the familiar thread-like leaves of 'Moonbeam Coreopsis.' Several pink cultivars have been introduced including two-toned 'Sweet Dreams' and 'Heaven's Gate'. Lucky southern gardeners can grow red 'Limerock Ruby'. Unlike the multitudes of yellow coreopsis, all pink coreopsis plants require consistent moisture.

Prairie Coreopsis (*C. palmata*) also called Stiff Coreopsis, has pale yellow flowers and matures at 12–30 inches tall. It is somewhat aggressive. Tall Coreopsis (*C. tripteris*) can become 6–8 feet tall, so this one needs to grow at the back of the border. It blooms in late summer to early fall.

PLANTING REQUIREMENTS
Coreopsis is a very forgiving plant and will grow nearly anywhere. It prefers average, well-drained soil in full sun. It will not tolerate a consistently wet planting site, nor does it bloom as well in shade.

PROPAGATION
Divide mature clumps in spring or fall, transplant seedlings, or plant ripened seed. This plant will also self-sow but is not hard to control.

Adam's Needle (*Yucca filamentosa* 'Color Guard')
Zones 4–10
30 inches
Flowers 6–8 feet
Blooms: Summer
White flowers
Deer and rabbit resistant

You may question including Yucca as a "front-of-the-garden" selection, but envision this unusual plant as a focal point in a front corner of the garden. Just give it enough space to show off its grandeur.

Some garden sites list Yuccas hardy only to Zone 5. However, it is reputedly hardy to −30 degrees so that makes it a Zone 4 plant. Right? Try it in any case. Or opt for one of the hardier new cultivars.

There are several new introductions for Zones 4–10. With 'Color Guard', wide bands of cream and white run through the center of each leaf. 'Bright Edge' has a very thin yellow margin. From its lighter green foliage, 'Ivory Tower' sends up spectacular 60-inch white flower spikes in midsummer. The sharp-edged leaves of 'Hofer Blue' are silvery-blue in spring, changing to a darker greenish-blue as the season progresses. 'Variegata', a smaller plant with creamy white edges, is hardy in Zones 5–10 and marginally hardy in Zone 4. It typically grows 18–24 inches with the flower stalk reaching 5 feet.

Rattlesnake Master (*Eryngium yuccifolium*) is a yucca lookalike. It grows 2–5 feet tall and has tall spikes of prickly, white, ball-like flowers that appear from June to September. This tallgrass prairie native is hardy in Zones 3–8. Its planting requirements and propagation are similar to *Yucca filamentosa*. It is on the recommended lists for rain gardens.

PLANTING REQUIREMENTS

Plant this drought-tolerant native of the Southeast in well-drained soil in full sun. Yucca will not bloom in shade and the roots will rot in poorly drained locations. Use a sharp knife to remove the blooming stalk at the base after bloom is complete. Bloom stalks can persist as "dead woody stalks" for 2–3 years. Cut back dead basal leaves in spring. It has a deep, woody root that is difficult to divide (or to remove, for that matter).

PROPAGATION

Remove small offshoots from the base of the mother plant in spring or fall and transplant. Plant fully ripened seeds. The Yucca moth is the pollinator of Yucca.

Medium: Middle of the Garden

Phlox (*Phlox paniculata*)

Zones 3–8
20–32 inches
Blooms: Summer
White or lavender flowers

The showy, upright, rosy-lavender or white panicles of our native phlox are well known to gardeners across the United States. And what a beautiful focal point it makes in a perennial garden! Butterflies and hummingbirds love its sweet nectar.

When the flowers fade, cut the stalks just below the flower head and phlox will bloom again in late summer or early fall. Keep the soil moist, especially in the heat of summer. Phlox dislikes drought.

Hundreds of sizes and colors are available as cultivars so sky and wallet are the only limits. My favorites include pure white 'David'; 'Lilac Flame'®, an 8–10 inch deep violet purple with a white eye; and 15-inch, bright red 'Red Riding Hood'. Mildew-resistant 'Lord Clayton' has rosy flowers set off by dark purple spring foliage that turns a lighter greenish-purple as the season progresses. If you want something truly unique, look for 18-inch 'Aureole'. Each bright, hot pink flower has a thin margin of chartreuse. And the petals of this amazing Jan Verschoor cultivar do not drop.

PLANTING REQUIREMENTS

Plant phlox in average to loamy, well-drained garden soil in full sun. Will accept shade, but does not bloom as profusely in less light. Likes moist soil, but not wet feet. Good air circulation is important to prevent mildew. Some cultivars are mildew resistant.

PROPAGATION

Divide mature clumps in spring or fall. Will self-sow, or plant ripened seed in the fall. Hybrids may not breed true, so for specific phlox cultivars, purchase from a nursery.

Butterfly Weed, aka Butterfly Milkweed (*Asclepias tuberosa*)

Zones 3–9

12–30 inches

Blooms: Summer

Drought tolerant

Deer resistant

Rain garden

How can anyone dislike Milkweed? I am totally enamored of the huge, flat flower heads in hot orange, bright yellow, rose, or pale lavender-pink. And if you plant them, you can be assured that Monarch butterflies will not be far behind. Bright orange Butterflyweed consistently hosts their wildly striped caterpillars. It is also a favorite nectar source of Diana and Fritillary butterflies as well as both Black and Tiger Swallowtails. The cultivar 'Hello Yellow' is 24–36 inches with large, flat, bright yellow flowers. It blooms late in the summer.

In late summer, the rosy-pink flowers of tall Swamp Milkweed (*A. incarnata*) bloom. No, not in the swamp or even in a particularly wet garden. Just in a normal perennial bed. This species is also a good choice for a rain garden. It gets to be 3–4 feet tall in my garden but can be taller in the wild.

I will confess that I even allow a clump of three tall shoots of Common Milkweed (*A. syriaca*) to grow in my front garden. Granted, it is a challenge to keep that giant under control because it spreads by vigorous rhizomes, but

I faithfully patrol the area and the surrounding grass to yank out new pale green shoots. They pull easily and do not return. They just pop up in another spot. But I can visit that clump anytime during the summer and find tiny Monarch eggs concealed under the huge rough leaves, caterpillars in all stages of development munching here and there, or even a beautiful, gold-studded, lime-green chrysalis. Monarchs flit about my yard all summer long.

I love to raise Monarchs from egg to butterfly on my kitchen counter in a big, glass, gallon jar. My grandchildren come faithfully to check on the progress, watching with delight as the tiny winged creature finally emerges, pumping its wings to full size.

Common Milkweed has attractive, large, pale, lavender-pink, ball-shaped flowers so although it is huge and can be aggressive without maintenance, it is a handsome plant. If you don't want to grow it, at least seek it out along the roadsides. With increased development it is harder and harder to find. To help keep our Monarch populations flourishing, add a few milkweed plants of some sort to your perennial bed. You will be glad you did!

PLANTING REQUIREMENTS
With few exceptions, Milkweeds demand well-drained soil. The long taproot will rot if the soil is consistently wet. Prairie Nursery in Wisconsin offers a "clay buster" that does better in heavy clay soils.

PROPAGATION
Milkweed produces long, spindle-shaped seedpods filled with silky filaments. Each filament holds a seed at the end. Clean the dried seeds in the fall and plant. Or transplant young seedlings, making sure to protect the fragile taproot. Once established they are difficult if not impossible to move.

Purple Coneflower (*Echinacea purpurea*)
Zones 3–8
15–30 inches
Blooms: Summer
Purple or rose-purple flowers
Drought tolerant
Deer resistant
Purple Coneflower is one of the treasured staples of the native perennial garden. In fact, it is a treasure in any garden. The hybridizers have had a field

day producing hundreds of unique cultivars from this accommodating native.

I will always grow the species as my first choice, but I have to admit to purchasing several interesting cultivars. I like many of the Big Sky introductions like golden-yellow 'Harvest Moon' with its spectacular orange dome in the center. My favorite is probably 'Rubinstern' (Ruby Star), an improved version of 'Magnus' with huge, hot pink ray flowers topped with a bronzy red dome. I also like the new introduction 'Pow Wow Wildberry', a 2010 AAS Winner. 'White Swan' is a beautifully drooping white selection. 'Lilliput' and 'Kim's Knee High' are both hardy dwarf cultivars great for the very front of the border.

I am not fond of cultivars with fluffy, double, meringue-like centers or ones that look like something from outer space. 'Double Decker' sports little ray flowers perching atop the raised spiny dome. 'Coral Reef' and 'Coconut Lime' are fascinating plants with unusual flowers, but they do not look like Coneflowers. Cultivars are fun, but as an old-fashioned native plant enthusiast, I want them to at least resemble the species.

Pale Purple Coneflower (*E. pallida*) blooms a little earlier than *E. purpurea*. The narrow lavender ray flowers have a pronounced droop.

PLANTING REQUIREMENTS
Plant in any average well-drained garden soil. Will do fine in sandy or clay soils, and tolerates mild drought or even wet feet for a while.

PROPAGATION
Divide mature clumps in spring or fall. Plant ripened seed in fall. Will self-sow but unwanted seedlings are not difficult to weed out. Or transplant them to another spot.

Blazing Star (*Liatris* spp.)
Zones 3–10
18–30 inches
Blooms: Midsummer to early fall
Lavender, purple, or violet flowers

Deer resistant

Rain garden

There are many species of Liatris, so for a longer bloom period, plant several. All are butterfly magnets with tall spires of bright purple-hued flowers and all are beautiful in the center of any sunny garden.

Blazing Star or Gayfeather (*Liatris spicata* L.) is the species most often found in garden centers. It sends up tall, narrow spikes of small, compact, feathery lavender flowers that resemble a bottlebrush blooming from the top down. Fastidious gardeners can clip the tops off spent flowers and still have a decent looking garden. 'Kobold' is 18 inches tall with lilac-purple flowers; 'Floristan Violet' is taller, maturing at 30 inches. Its flowers have a rosy hue. 'Floristan White' is one of the few whites available, but they are more accurately described as off-white. The plant gets to be 36 inches tall.

Dense Blazing Star (*L. punctata* Hook.), also called Dotted Blazing Star, has lovely, raggedy, violet-purple flowers. A smaller Liatris, it has speckled leaves.

Meadow Blazing Star (*L. ligulistylis*) grows 12–24 inches tall in the garden. The soft, fluffy flowers have a rosy hue and march up the stiff stems, branching as they rise. Monarch butterflies flock to these pretty, nectar-rich flowers. This is my favorite Liatris. It is a beautiful floral specimen, but is not easy to find in the nursery trade. If you cannot locate it locally, check out one of the native-plant mail-order nurseries.

Rough Blazing Star (*L. aspera*) has flower spikes with individual rosy-purple flowers that resemble soft, fluffy, round buttons. It forms a clump and blooms late in the season. It can be short-lived, but is worth having if even for a limited time.

Prairie Blazing Star (*L. pycnostachya*) can reach 6 feet tall. Tall flowering wands of flowers in shades of pink and lavender cover the tall, stiff stems in late summer. This particular Liatris is a favored roadside planting choice of the Department of Transportation (DOT) in several states and can form large colonies in the wild.

PLANTING REQUIREMENTS

Liatris prefers average, well-drained soil and does better in soil that is not overly rich or moist. In too much shade it will flop and does not bloom well.

PROPAGATION

This plant grows from a tuberous rootstock rather than the usual fibrous perennial roots. These can be divided like peonies or potatoes, making sure each section has an eye. The eyes should not be planted too deeply or the plant will not bloom. Worse yet, it may die.

It will self-sow; seedlings can be carefully transplanted. It takes 2–3 years for these to reach blooming size.

Cardinal Flower (*Lobelia cardinalis*)

Zones 2–9
24–30 inches
Blooms: Midsummer to early fall
Bright red flowers
Deer resistant
Rain garden

Brilliant red flowers make this plant a standout for the perennial garden. It loves a sunny location as long as there is adequate moisture in the soil. In hot, humid zones, gardeners may want to provide afternoon shade unless the soil is kept consistently moist. Hummingbirds zoom around the bright flowers and several Swallowtail butterflies seek out the nectar.

Cultivars include 'Alba', a white-flowered cultivar, and 'Twilight Zone' (pink). 'Bees Flame' has scarlet red flowers and deep, bronzy red foliage. It is a knockout. 'Fried Green Tomatoes' has tomato red flowers and burgundy-brown spring foliage that turns greenish-purple as the season progresses. These newest cultivars may only be available through mail order, but be the squeaky wheel at your local nursery. They are outstanding plants.

PLANTING REQUIREMENTS

Plant Cardinal Flower in moist, well-drained, rich, loamy soil in full sun or part shade. It is a good rain garden plant and enjoys being kept consistently moist. The only disadvantage to Cardinal Flower is that it can be short-lived.

PROPAGATION

Transplant young seedlings or divide mature plants in spring or fall. It will grow from seed.

Royal Catchfly (*Silene regia*)

Zones 4–7
2–4 feet
Blooms: Midsummer
Bright red flowers
Deer and rabbit resistant
Rain garden

Royal Catchfly may be another red plant to add to your fiery native arsenal! This stunning native is a short-lived perennial but self-sows readily. It is on both the threatened and endangered species lists. The U.S. Fish and Wildlife Service defines endangered species as species at the brink of extinction now. Threatened species are likely to be at the brink in the near future. However, *Silene regia* is easy to grow from seed and once established will self-sow, so this is one way native plant gardeners can help to preserve a particular endangered species.

Fire Pink *(S. virginica)* is another brilliant red-flowering native. Hardy in Zones 4–8, it grows 2–3 feet tall. The flower petals are notched. Fire Pink was proposed as the state flower of Indiana to replace the Asian peony, but the bill died in committee.

PLANTING REQUIREMENTS

Royal Catchfly and Fire Pink both grow in average, well-drained soil. Royal Catchfly prefers full sun. I have seen it growing at the edge of an alley in sand and gravel, so it does not need rich loam. However it requires good drainage. With soggy clay soil the taproot may rot. Fire Pink is a woodland-edge plant and grows best in part sun/part shade.

PROPAGATION

Transplant young seedlings or grow from seed. Plant ripened seed in fall near the mother plant to create a mass. Cold stratify seed for four weeks for indoor planting.

Blue Vervain (*Verbena hastata*)

Zones 3–8
2–5 feet
Blooms: Midsummer to late fall
Purple-blue flowers

Deer resistant

Rain garden

Blue Vervain is a clump-forming perennial with spiky blue or purple-blue flower stalks. This square-stemmed plant can spread aggressively. It occasionally grows as tall as 6 feet in the wild, but does not generally get taller than 2–3 feet in the home perennial bed. It is a good choice for the middle of the garden. Deadhead for longer blooming period. Blue Vervain is a larval host and nectar source for Common Buckeye butterflies.

Nurseries offer 'Blue Spires' (violet-blue), 'Pink Spires' (rosy-lavender), 'White Spires' (white), and 'Purple Spires' (purple).

Hoary Vervain (*V. stricta*) is a somewhat short-lived perennial with large, light blue flowers and coarse, fuzzy leaves. More suited to the back of the garden, it blooms from July to August. It is hardy in Zones 4–9. This species is another DOT favorite for roadside plantings.

PLANTING REQUIREMENTS

Vervain does well when planted in average, moist soil with good drainage in full sun. It prefers consistent moisture and thrives in a ⬤ rain garden.

PROPAGATION

Plant seeds in the fall. Seeds need cold stratification to germinate.

Tall: Back of the Garden

Gray-headed Coneflower (*Ratibida pinnata*)

Zones 3–8

3–5 feet

Blooms: Summer

Yellow flowers

Drought tolerant

Deer resistant

Rain garden

Also called Yellow Coneflower, this native perennial is recommended by prairie restoration experts as one of the first to bloom in a new prairie. The bright yellow ray flowers droop from a tall, cone-like head that is greenish-gray in spring, darkening with age to dark brown. These heads smell faintly of anise if bruised or crushed. Plant a mass of these in the middle or back of the garden to get the most bang for your buck.

Mexican Hat or Prairie Coneflower (*R. columnifera*) grows only 12 to 18 inches tall, blooming from June to September. The unique flowers with tall, brown cones and colorful yellow, red, or red-edged-with-yellow flower petals supposedly resemble Mexican sombreros. They are an interesting addition to the garden, and unlike the tall Gray-headed Coneflower, can be grown close to the front of the border.

PLANTING REQUIREMENTS
These forgiving natives will thrive in average, well-drained soil, loamy soil, or even clay. Ratibida species love full sun and will bloom longer and stand taller than those living in shadier spots.

PROPAGATION
Both of these coneflowers self-sow or ripened seed can be planted in fall for spring germination. Dividing mature clumps in fall is possible, but there are usually enough seedlings to make this task unnecessary. Plants bloom the second year.

Purple Prairie Clover (*Dalea purpurea*)
Zones 3–8
18–24 inches
Blooms: Summer
Violet-rose flowers
Drought tolerant
Deer resistant
Rock garden
Purple Prairie Clover resembles Mexican Hat in habit but is an entirely different species. It is taller than Mexican Hat, sometimes growing as tall as 3 feet. Instead of a single "brim" of yellow ray flowers, rings of rosy-purple flowers with hints of gold bloom from the bottom to the top, putting on their show in summer. Prairie clover fixes nitrogen in the soil and has a deep taproot that can delve five to six feet deep. Formerly known as *Petalostemon purpureum*, *Dalea purpurea* is a popular choice for native prairie restoration projects. Mass Prairie Clover for best effect.

White Prairie Clover *(D. candida)* has the same basic requirements and looks the same except for the flower color.

PLANTING REQUIREMENTS

Prefers average, well-drained soil in full sun. Poor drainage will rot the deep taproot.

PROPAGATION

Prairie Clover seeds readily. Seed planted in spring will produce young seedlings in the same growing season. Transplant young seedlings. Or allow seeds to ripen and dry on flowering plants and plant in the fall. This native will self-sow with most young plants germinating near the mother. Division of mature plants is not usually successful due to the deep taproot.

Michigan Lily *(Lilium michiganense)*
Turk's Cap Lily *(L. superbum)*

Zones 3–9
3–6 feet
Blooms: Summer
Orange flowers

Michigan Lily's spotted, nodding, bright orange flowers grow in a whorl at the top of a long, stiff stem. Unlike most lilies, the six-part flowers curve backward, which is why it is sometimes confused with Turk's Cap *(L. superbum)*. Michigan Lily's flowers bend so far back, they nearly touch the stem. The leaves are evenly arranged around the stiff stems.

The orange flowers of Turk's Cap *(L. superbum)* bend backward but also upward. It is taller and more robust than Michigan Lily. Michigan Lily has yellow bulbs; Turk's Cap bulbs are white. Both of these lilies attract butterflies and hummingbirds.

PLANTING REQUIREMENTS

Plant in average, well-drained soil. These lilies prefer full sun and slightly moist soil, so it helps to mulch the roots.

PROPAGATION

Plant bulbs 5–8 inches deep. Smaller bulbs can be separated from the main bulb but it is easiest to purchase bulbs from a reliable nursery or bulb catalog. Do not dig either of these from the wild.

Bee Balm (*Monarda* spp.)

Zones 3–8

3–5 feet

Blooms: Summer

Red, lavender, white, or pink flowers

Deer resistant

Rain garden

This species, a member of the mint family, spreads quite aggressively by rhizomes. To keep it tidy in the garden, divide plants every two or three years. It is slightly aromatic and attracts birds and butterflies. For a particular flower color in the garden, choose a specific species. I have grown red, lavender, hot pink, pale pink, and white Bee Balms. I prefer the brightly colored reds or pinks and plant them in a mass to brighten up a corner of the garden.

Oswego Tea (*M. didyma*) has shaggy, brilliant red flowers complemented by bright green leaves. It will grow under Black Walnut trees and accepts part shade, although it does best in full sun. The Chicago Botanic Garden has done extensive testing and breeding for mildew resistance: 'Gardenview Scarlet' (red-rose), 'Jacob Cline' (one of the best reds), 'Petite Delight' (12–15-inch lavender-rose), 'Blaukranz' (hot pink), and 'Colrain Red' (unusually shaped violet-red flowers) all made their recommended list.

Wild Bergamot (*M. fistulosa* L.) has pink or pale lavender flowers and is generally considered the native prairie species. It is often chosen for DOT roadside plantings.

Spotted Bee Balm (*M. punctata*) has lavender-pink or yellow whorled bracts. Also known as Spotted Horsemint, it blooms in early summer (June–July) and is a shorter species, maturing at 18–24 inches. It is a biennial and sometimes even considered an annual, but self-sows readily. 'Fantasy' has pale yellow flowers with purple spots.

PLANTING REQUIREMENTS

Plant in average, well-drained garden soil in full or part sun. Provide adequate ventilation to prevent powdery mildew. Several new cultivars have been bred to be mildew resistant.

PROPAGATION

Divide mature plants in spring or fall, plant ripened brown seeds in fall, or cold stratify to plant in spring. This plant readily self-sows and will also spread slowly by runners, so additional propagation is not generally necessary unless you want to share a start or seeds with a friend.

Culver's Root (*Veronicastrum virginicum*)
Zones 3–8
3–6 feet
Blooms: Summer
White flowers
Drought tolerant
Deer resistant
Rain garden

I grow this plant at the back of the garden. The tall, white, candelabra spires look graceful while in full bloom. Elegant, textured, green leaves grow in whorls around a stiff stalk. For a spectacular summer show, mass several together.

'Album' has snowy white flowers, 'Apollo' sports shades of lavender and purple, and 'Fascination' has lavender-rose flowers. A lovely pink form called 'Pink Glow' is also available.

PLANTING REQUIREMENTS
Keep plants growing in full sun consistently moist or the leaves will turn an unsightly yellow. It doesn't hurt the plant, but it is unattractive. Leave the flower stalks on over winter to promote self-seeding.

PROPAGATION
Divide in spring or fall, or sow ripened seed in fall. Moist stratify and plant in the spring. Take root cuttings in the fall. Be sure each has a bud.

Queen of the Prairie (*Filipendula rubra*)
Zones 3–9
3–6 feet
Blooms: Summer
Pink flowers
Sun/part sun
Deer resistant
Rain garden

When Queen of the Prairie sends up that tall spike of pink, fluffy flowers high above its bright green leaves, it outshines every other plant in the garden. With flower heads that are 4–10 inches across and nearly a foot long, this beautiful native plant makes quite a statement when it is in full bloom, Envision several plants creating a large mass. wow!

'Venusta Magnifica' has deeper pink flowers.

Spent flower heads dry to a nice tan similar to astilbe plumes, so I usually let them remain in place for continued interest. They will not rebloom with deadheading.

PLANTING REQUIREMENTS

Plant in rich, loamy, well-drained garden soil that is consistently moist in full sun for best results. It will also perform in part sun.

PROPAGATION

Queen of the Prairie will self-sow if left to its own devices. Divide mature clumps in spring or plant ripened seeds.

Anise Hyssop (*Agastache foeniculum*)

Zones 4–8

24–48 inches

Blooms: Summer to late fall

Drought tolerant

Deer and rabbit resistant

A member of the mint family, Anise Hyssop sends up a lavender-purple flower spike that can be 8 inches high. This tall plant, reaching as high as 4 feet, smells like anise or licorice when bruised. Deadhead to extend the blooms until frost.

The cultivar 'Golden Jubilee' has bright gold leaves followed by 3–4-inch intensely purple flower spikes. It was a 2003 AAS Winner. This shorter cultivar appreciates a little extra water during drought. It is hardy in Zones 5–8.

PLANTING REQUIREMENTS

Thrives in average, well-drained soil. It will tolerate drought but resents overwatering. Grows best in full sun but will tolerate part shade.

PROPAGATION

Divide in spring or fall. Plant ripened seeds in fall. Root stem-cuttings in spring from new growth. Will self-sow.

FALL

Short: Front of the Garden

Bottle Gentian (*Gentiana andrewsii*)

Zones 3–7

12–24 inches

Blooms: Late summer to fall

Purple, blue, or cream flowers

Sun/Shade

This plant may be difficult to obtain except through mail order sources, native plant society or garden club sales, or from a good friend. I got mine from the latter and it has flourished in my Minnesota garden, rewarding me with electric blue or royal purple closed buds that never open even though they stay colorful for a month. How do big, fat bumblebees pry open the tightly closed flower, climb in, and pollinate it? It's a mystery to me!

My plant gets sun most of the day, along with some afternoon shade. There is a rare one with creamy white flowers (*G. alba*), but I prefer the purple/blue color. Unfortunately, deer and rabbits consider the flowers of Bottle Gentian a tasty treat, so take precautions or there will be no beautiful blue "buds" in your garden until next fall. Some report having difficulty establishing gentian, but once it deems your selected spot worthy, it just returns year after year.

PLANTING REQUIREMENTS

Gentian requires a moist planting site. Loamy, humus-rich, well-drained soil is ideal. Provide additional moisture during times of drought or extreme heat.

PROPAGATION

This plant grows from a crown. Divide crowns in fall or early spring. After peak bloom, the closed flowers will turn tan and the enclosed seeds will ripen. Sprinkle ripened seed on the ground in the fall and cover lightly, or cold stratify them for at least three months and plant in early spring. Success from seeds can be challenging so I recommend purchasing the plants from a reliable source. Do not dig from the wild.

Great Blue Lobelia (*Lobelia siphilitica* L.)

Zones 4–9

24–30 inches

Blooms: Late summer to fall

Blue or violet-blue flowers

Sun/part shade

Deer resistant

Rain garden

Delicate, blue flowers with pointed "lips" (two lobes above and three below) look like a duplicate of the brilliant red flowers of its sibling, Cardinal Flower. Great Blue Lobelia blooms slightly longer and survives more reliably in the garden than Cardinal Flower.

'Lilac Candles' is an 18-inch compact dwarf. 'Rose Beacon' is a gardenworthy hybrid with rosy-pink flowers.

PLANTING REQUIREMENTS

Needs a consistently moist planting site and does not tolerate drought. It does best in sun or part sun; it will tolerate shady spots although the plants may be more floppy.

PROPAGATION

Lift and transplant ground-hugging rosettes in spring or fall, divide mature clumps, transplant self-sown seedlings, or plant seed in fall. The seed needs moist stratification to germinate. Plant treated seeds in spring.

Aster (*Symphyotrichum* spp.)

Zones 3–8

Blooms: Late summer to fall

Blue, purple, pink, or white flowers

Deer resistant

Rain garden

Note the botanical name change from simply *Aster* to *Symphyotrichum*. Easier to remember? Oh well . . .

A mainstay in the fall garden, asters offer a variety of flower colors. Mature plants may be only a few inches tall to 8-foot giants. (Taller species are described later in the medium and tall sections). In this "short" section are common short aster species such as Sky Blue Aster, Smooth Blue Aster, and white Heath Aster.

I have also included several of the popular cultivars from our tall familiar New England Aster. These low, compact cultivars are lovely in the fall garden. Most are drought tolerant and are hardy in Zones 3–8 unless noted otherwise. Some begin to bloom in mid- to late August, but most are at their peak in September and October. Asters perform best in full sun.

Bushy Aster (*S. dumosum* aka *Aster dumosus*) is a dwarf, lilac-blue or white aster also known as Michaelmas Daisy. It grows 12–24 inches tall, has narrow green leaves, and blooms from August to October. The 12–16-inch 'Wood's' cultivars come from this species including 'Wood's Light Blue', 'Wood's Pink', 'Wood's Blue', and 'Wood's Purple.'

Sky Blue Aster (*S. oolentangiense* aka *A. azureus*) will get rave reviews in the fall garden. Gorgeous, violet-blue, daisy-like flowers with bright yellow disc centers bloom on 18–24 inch plants. If rosy-purple flowers are what you prefer, search for Silky Aster (*S. sericeus*).

Smooth Blue Aster (*S. laeve*) is taller, maturing at 24–48 inches. It has pale lavender flowers with yellow centers and is the nectar and larval food source for the Pearl Crescent butterfly. 'Bluebird' was introduced by Dr. Richard Lighty of the Mt. Cuba Center. It grows three feet tall and has exceptionally large lavender flowers. Pinch it in early summer; a compact, bushy plant is less likely to flop during flowering.

Aromatic Aster (*S. oblongifolium*) has lavender flowers. Crushed leaves emit a fragrance. The bushy 'October Skies' is a 2-foot plant covered with delicate blue flowers. This pretty cultivar loves to run and spread. All bloom in the fall.

Heath Aster (*S. ericoides*) Small white asters that pop up here and there and everywhere in the fall are probably Heath Asters. They are usually 12–30 inches tall. 'Blue Star' Heath Aster has a better, more compact form than the species. Pretty, pale, powder blue flowers with hints of white densely cover this 18–24-inch cultivar in September and October. The daisy-like flowers have bright yellow centers.

'Snow Flurry' only grows about 6 inches tall. Its dense mats will serve as a ground cover. I planted it at the front of a border and love the effect. If it gets carried away, I dig and transplant the errant ones in another spot. It is not hard to maintain.

Cultivars of New England Aster (*S. novae-angliae*) include my favorite, 'Purple Dome'. Vibrant purple flowers cover the 18-inch compact plant in fall. Tiny 'Purple Pixie' only reaches 12–18 inches with similar flowers. 'Vibrant Dome' is a hot pink, 20-inch sport of 'Purple Dome'. Description of the full-sized New England Aster appears later in this chapter.

PLANTING REQUIREMENTS
Plant in average, well-drained garden soil in full sun. I routinely sprinkle Milorganite fertilizer around and over my 'Purple Dome' asters to prevent rabbit damage to new spring foliage.

PROPAGATION
Divide mature plants in spring or fall, sow seeds in fall, transplant self-sown seedlings.

Turtlehead (*Chelone* spp.)
Zones 3–9
24–36 inches
Blooms: Midsummer to fall
White, pink, or lavender-pink flowers
Deer resistant
Rain garden
Snapdragon-like flowers resembling the head of a turtle march up and down the rigid stems of Turtlehead. I have large clumps of Pink Turtlehead (*C. obliqua* var. *speciosa*) growing in my garden and absolutely love the soft lavender-pink flowers. I also grow White Turtlehead (*C. glabra*), with pretty, pink-tinged white flowers. Both bloom happily in two spots. One garden is in full sun, the other in part shade, and there are no complaints from either area as long as there is sufficient moisture. Turtlehead is the larval food source for the Baltimore Checkerspot butterfly. 'Black Ace' is a dark-leaved form of White Turtlehead.

Another gardenworthy Pink Turtlehead is *C. lyonii,* a native of the southeastern United States. The 30-inch tall cultivar 'Hot Lips' is from this species. It has intensely rose-pink flowers and glossy green leaves. It is a beauty.

PLANTING REQUIREMENTS

Turtlehead demands moist soil and although it will tolerate some dryness, it will perish in extreme drought, so keep it well watered in the heat of summer especially if your plants are in full sun. Mass plants 12–18 inches apart for the best effect.

PROPAGATION

Separate mature clumps, working the fibrous rhizomes apart with your hands in early spring or fall, and plant immediately. Plant ripened seed in fall. Turtlehead self-sows, but seeds take a year to germinate and two to flower, so purchasing plants is the best plan for impatient gardeners.

Virginia Mountain Mint (*Pycnanthemum virginianum*)

Zones 3–7

12–30 inches

Blooms: Midsummer to fall

White flowers

Deer resistant

Butterflies and beneficial insects flock to this member of the mint family. Virginia Mountain Mint can be aggressive in rich soil so do not pamper this bushy, white-flowering herb. The flower buds make a tasty tea.

Slender Mountain Mint (*P. tenuifolium*) is an airy plant and blooms slightly earlier in the season. It has fine, narrow leaves, branches more than Virginia Mountain Mint, and has delicate white flowers. It grows 12–36 inches tall.

Plants in the mint family tend to spread and create colonies so depending on your perennial garden, this may not be the best or most maintenance-free choice, but the white flowers are pretty and attract butterflies. It may be a good choice as a ground cover in a wild spot.

PLANTING REQUIREMENTS

Mountain Mint generally grows in moist locations in the wild, but will grow in just about any type of soil including average garden soil in full or partial sun. It is tolerant of clay soil.

PROPAGATION

Mint species take care of their own propagation! However, gardeners can easily take divisions in spring or fall.

Rose Mallow (*Hibiscus moscheutos* L.)

Zones 4–9

3–6 feet

Blooms: Midsummer to fall

Creamy white flowers

Deer resistant

Granted, Rose Mallow is not a small front-of-the-garden plant, but the huge flowers scream for attention, so what better place is there for these tropical looking beauties than at the front? Dinner-plate sized blooms guarantee oohs and aahs. The species flowers are creamy white with vibrant, burgundy-red eyes surrounding the yellow stamens.

'Jazzberry Jam' has raspberry flowers, 'Lord Baltimore' is crimson red, and 3–4-foot-tall 'Kopper King' has incredible, coppery red flowers and outstanding maroon leaves. 'Turn of the Century' is one of my favorites, with bicolored flowers in shades of red and pink. Create a corner focal point with some of these spectacular plants.

PLANTING REQUIREMENTS

Plant in well-drained, average soil in full sun and provide adequate moisture, especially during the heat of summer. Remember that this plant is really late to emerge so do not give up—or inadvertently dig it up. And give it plenty of room. Some gardeners plant slow-growing dwarf evergreens in front of these tall plants.

PROPAGATION

Divide existing plants to get the same plant. Hybrids do not breed true, or can be sterile and not even set seeds. Seeds from the species can be planted in the fall.

Medium: Middle of the Garden

Goldenrod (*Solidago* spp.)

Zones 3–9

30–48 inches

Blooms: Late summer to fall

Yellow flowers

Deer resistant

Rain garden

Goldenrod species abound, but only the clump-forming types are suitable for the home garden. Goldenrods bloom from August through October, so plant more than one variety for longer lasting results. Deadheading extends bloom on all *Solidago* species. Butterflies, bees, and many other beneficial insects seek out Goldenrod flowers. And no, it doesn't cause hay fever. For that, blame Ragweed (*Ambrosia* spp.) with its airborne pollen that releases about the same time that goldenrod species bloom.

Showy Goldenrod (*S. speciosa*) is the best choice for spectacular flowers. Bright yellow spires stand tall on dark reddish stems above this striking, clump-forming perennial. It only grows about 4 feet tall in my garden, but in an ideal spot it can stretch to 5 feet.

Rough-stemmed Goldenrod (*S. rugosa*) tolerates more soil moisture than other goldenrod species. Another clump-former, this 24–30 inch tall native sends up golden sprays in late summer that make quite a show for several weeks. Deadheading will extend the bloom. 'Fireworks' is more compact than the species and looks just like its name—exploding fireworks. The Plant Delights catalog describes 'Lynn Lowrey' as *Solidago* 'Fireworks' on steroids. For 12–18-inch introductions, look for 'Little Lemon' or 'Sweety'. The latter is the smallest. Both of these little cultivars have clusters of bright lemon yellow flowers that just glow at the front of the border.

Stiff Goldenrod (*Oligoneuron rigidum* aka *Solidago rigida*) has recently been reassigned to the *Oligoneuron* genus. Each impressive bunch of flowers resembles a big, yellow-gold bouquet. This 2–5-foot-tall species has large, light green leaves that feel like soft felt. The tall main flower stem is hairy. Deer and rabbits enjoy the new foliage. It grows from rhizomes and tends to be weedier in the garden than the previous species so, although its flowers are impressive, Stiff Goldenrod may be a better choice for a less formal planting space.

PLANTING REQUIREMENTS

Plant goldenrod in average, well-drained garden soil in full or part sun. It is drought tolerant and attracts beneficial insects to its nectar-rich flowers. Most goldenrods are deer resistant.

PROPAGATION

Divide young plants in spring or fall. Mature plants may be difficult to divide or transplant due to their deep root systems. Self-sows. Transplant seedlings or plant seed in the fall.

Sneezeweed (*Helenium autumnale*)

Zones 3–8
30–48 inches
Blooms: Midsummer to fall
Yellow flowers
Rain garden

Long-blooming Sneezeweed elicits rave reviews for its unusual flowers. A fat center dome of dull yellow disc flowers is ringed with rays of bright yellow, daisy-like ray flowers with spaces between them. The rays are shaped like small, scalloped-edged wedges. An upright plant with a fibrous root system, it can be useful for streamside erosion control. Sneezeweed gets its name because at one time it was used as an ingredient in snuff. However, there is no evidence that it actually causes sneezing. On the website About.com (August 2010), Marie Iannotti comments, "Helenium looks like a daisy dipped in M&M colors."

'Mardi Gras' is as wild and exciting as its name, with multicolored shades of brilliant orange, red, and yellow. It grows 36–40 inches tall in my garden and blooms for weeks. Another favorite, 'Moerheim Beauty', has orangey red centers with matching flowers tipped with yellow. 'Ruby Tuesday' and 'Rubinzwerg' both have scarlet to coppery red flowers with shades of brown and yellow in their chubby, domed centers. A double-flowering form, 'Double Trouble', with an amazing number of beautiful yellow petals, is striking but does not resemble the species at all!

PLANTING REQUIREMENTS

Plant in average, somewhat moist, well-drained soil. Provide additional moisture in the heat of summer. Heleniums will tolerate clay soil but do not like drought. Deadhead to prolong bloom.

PROPAGATION

If possible, divide the fibrous-rooted existing clumps in spring. Plant ripened seeds of the species in fall. Helenium will self-sow, but seedlings from cultivars and hybrids will probably not resemble the mother plant.

Obedient Plant (*Physostegia virginiana*)

Zones 2–9
18–30 inches
Blooms: Midsummer to fall
Lavender-blue, pink, or white flowers
Deer resistant
Rain garden

Large clusters of tubular, lavender-blue flowers reminiscent of snapdragons bloom atop these clump-forming perennials. Change the position of a flower on its stalk and it will stay there until you move it again, hence the common name. However, Obedient Plant is anything but obedient in another respect. It will not stay where you plant it, but tears all over the garden. It even pokes its stems into another plant's space so that weeding it out becomes difficult. Its handsome flowers bloom in mid- to late summer when the garden is winding down. It can thrive in difficult planting sites, and will fill the bottom of a filtration basin or rain garden without hesitation, so it can be helpful in certain situations. To make Obedient Plant behave in a formal perennial border, plant it in a pot to curtail its rambunctious nature.

Gardeners who prefer more restrained perennials should consider 'Miss Manners', an 18–24-inch, well-behaved, white cultivar less inclined to spread. 'Alba' and 'Crystal Peak' are other compact white-flowering forms. 'Variegata', as the name implies, has green leaves edged with creamy white. For hot pink flowers, look for 'Vivid'.

PLANTING REQUIREMENTS
Plant in moist, well-drained average garden soil in full sun. Prune back 1/3 in early summer to make the plant more bushy and bloom a bit later in the season. If self-sowing is not desired, cut off the flower heads before they go to seed.

PROPAGATION
Divide mature plants in spring or fall, or plant ripe seed in fall. This member of the mint family self-sows and spreads aggressively by rhizomes.

Ironweed (*Vernonia noveboracensis*)
Zones 4–9
3–5 feet
Blooms: Fall
Purple flowers
Drought tolerant
Deer resistant
Rain garden
It is impossible to ignore this statuesque plant waving high above the garden. Ironweed has royal purple flowers and large serrated leaves. Plant a mob of yellow composite flowers around it for that opposite-on-the-color-wheel pop. Ironweed is one of the few plants that will survive under Black Walnut trees. Popular with butterflies and small birds, it will tolerate clay soil.

Ironweed is a plant you either love or hate. Herbivores do not eat it so it "stands like iron" to the frustration of farmers and ranchers who do not appreciate the bright purple flowers. As it ages, Ironweed also develops "rusty iron" stems, spent flowers, and seeds. Once established, it is there to stay, so choose the planting site wisely.

PLANTING REQUIREMENTS
Plant in average well-drained soil in full sun. Ironweed enjoys adequate moisture and is not fond of drought. For shorter, bushier plants, cut back sharply in spring.

PROPAGATION
Divide young plants in spring or late fall or plant ripe seeds in fall. Will self-sow.

New England Aster
(*Symphyotrichum novae-angliae* aka *Aster novae-angliae*)
Zones 3–9
3–4 feet
Blooms: Late summer to fall
Blue-violet flowers
Deer resistant
Rain garden

Fall blooming New England Asters look airy in my garden. When I pinch my plants back in early summer, they seldom grow taller than 4 feet. Shorter, bushier plants are less apt to require staking. I left a few unpinched specimens in the middle of my garden, but I am moving them to the back because the foliage does not remain pristine and they flop late in the season. Taller plants behind them should provide stability.

The yellow-centered multiple ray flowers of New England Asters are bigger and fuller than typical daisy-like flowers. I love the multiple flowers in shades of violet, purple, pink, blue, and even white that shimmer gently in the breeze above the narrow leaves. Butterflies enjoy the sweet nectar.

Unfortunately deer will nibble New England Aster, especially in early spring, even though it may not be their favorite munchable. New cultivars are particularly at risk. Use Milorganite. Deer hate the smell!

New York Aster (*S. novi-belgii*) matures at 3–4 feet with light blue flowers. Many popular smaller aster cultivars come from this species including 'Alert' (red to hot pink), 'Henry III' (lavender-mauve), and 'Professor Kippenburg' (light blue). 'Andenken an Alma Potschke' is a 4-foot-tall favorite in my garden with bright hot pink flowers. Alma is a late bloomer but her flowers are worth waiting for each fall. New York Aster is reputed to be deer resistant.

Heart-Leaved Aster (*S. cordifolium*) is also called common Blue Wood Aster. Delicate flowers of pale blue float like clouds above serrated green leaves. This aster thrives in part sun or light shade. The flowers are darker blue in more sunlight.

PLANTING REQUIREMENTS

Plant asters in moist to average, well-drained soil in full sun. Provide good air circulation around the plants. Overcrowding can cause powdery mildew. Cut to the ground after blooming to keep self-sowing to a minimum. New England Aster will grow in clay soil.

PROPAGATION

Divide young clumps in spring or fall, transplant seedlings, or sow ripe seed in the fall. Self-sows, but most asters are not invasive.

Boneset (*Eupatorium perfoliatum*)

Zones 3–9

3–5 feet

Blooms: Late summer to fall

White flowers

Deer resistant

Loose clusters of delicate white flowers bloom above rigid hairy stems that appear to poke through the large coarse leaves. However, the historic value of this perfoliate plant may be the best reason to acquire it. It is fun to have an unusual plant to talk about. Before the era of modern medicine, Boneset was widely used to treat infections such as flu or the common cold. Early settlers suffering from Bonebreak Fever often shook so hard they were "like to break their bones." A bitter-tasting tea made from Boneset supposedly stopped the shaking.

Some pioneer doctors prescribed the tea to patients after setting a broken bone. Nineteenth-century *Materia Medica* volumes on my historian husband's bookshelves discuss the uses of Boneset at length. Websites indicate that testing and experimentation with Boneset continues. In any case, this plant will elicit discussion.

PLANTING REQUIREMENTS

Plant in average, well-drained soil in full or part sun.

PROPAGATION

Divide young plants in early spring or sow ripe seeds in the fall. Will self-sow.

Tall: Back of the Garden

White Doll's Eye Aster (*Boltonia asteroides*)

Zones 3–9
Height 5–6 feet
Blooms: Late summer to fall
White flowers
Drought tolerant
Deer resistant

White Doll's Eye Aster is also called Boltonia or False Aster, and it does resemble the well-known fall aster. In mid- to late summer, bright white, daisy-like flowers with yellow centers bloom profusely, often continuing until frost.

False Chamomile *(B. asteroides* var. *latisquama)* also grows 5–6 feet tall with a slightly larger, yellow-centered, lavender-purple flower. It is also known as *Boltonia latisquama.*

'Pink Beauty', hardy in Zones 4–9, is shorter than the species, generally maturing at 3–5 feet. It has pale pink flowers with yellow centers. Its bloom period is a little shorter than the species.

'Snowbank' is a short, white-flowering, 3–4-foot cultivar, also hardy in Zones 4–9. If it is really feeling vigorous, it can stretch as high as 5–6 feet.

PLANTING REQUIREMENTS

Thrives in average well-drained soil. It will also tolerate clay soil. Pinch back in late spring or early summer if you desire bushiness. Provide full sun to prevent flopping. Staking is unnecessary in full sun.

PROPAGATION

Spreads by creeping rhizomes. Sow ripened seed in the fall or divide mature plants in fall or spring. Division is recommended every 3–4 years to keep the plants tidy.

Purple-stemmed Aster (*Symphyotrichum puniceum* aka *Aster puniceus*)

Zones 3–9
1–6 feet
Blooms: Late summer to late fall

Lavender flowers

Deer resistant

Rain garden

Purple-Stemmed Aster has a variety of common names including Swamp Aster, Bristly Aster, and Glossy-Leaved Aster. Like New England Aster, it has large, delicate, lavender-blue flowers and narrow leaves that clasp sturdy stems. It can also grow as tall as New England Aster—up to 6 feet—but it prefers a wetter site. The stem is usually hairy with a reddish-purple tint, but it can also be smooth and green, so stem color is not an absolute identifying characteristic. Purple-Stemmed Aster attracts many beneficial insects and is a larval food source for the Pearl Crescent and Silvery Checkerspot butterflies.

PLANTING REQUIREMENTS

Requires moist soil and tolerates wet sites so this may be a better choice for gardeners facing moisture challenges. It is good for a rain garden. It will bloom profusely well into fall, sometimes for as long as two months. Plant in full sun or it will flop.

PROPAGATION

Divide in spring or early fall, or sow ripened seeds.

Joe-pye Weed (*Eutrochium* spp.)

Zones 4–9

2–7 feet

Blooms: Late summer to fall

Pink or mauve flowers

Deer resistant

Rain garden

Previously both Joe-pye Weed and Boneset were listed in the genus *Eupatorium*. Recently the genus name of all Joe-pye Weeds was changed to *Eutrochium*. The new nomenclature is used in this section. In some sources Joe-pye Weed is identified as *Eupatoriadelphus purpureus* L. as well as the more familiar *Eupatorium purpureum*. Note that the species names remain the same.

This stately plant treated many ailments including typhoid fever. Most Joe-pye Weeds are hardy in Zones 4–9 and have mauve or dusty rose flowers. They grow equally well in full sun and part shade as long as there is adequate moisture. Joe-pye Weed is one of the most statuesque plants available for the back of the garden. Standing tall and regal, it fills the area with huge, soft, rounded flower clusters that command attention. The Missouri Botanical Garden's Encyclopedia of Life (EOL) website (eol.org) details the numbers of leaves in each whorl, the type of stem, and the recent change in scientific nomenclature. Hopefully this will make accurate identification easier.

Sweet Joe-pye Weed (*E. purpureum*) has 3–4 large, whorled leaves that clasp the solid, light green, hairless stems. The stem branches near the top to hold large, domed clusters of mauve-pink flowers that are attractive to butterflies and beneficial insects. The stalks holding the flowers may be slightly hairy. Sweet Joe-pye Weed grows 3–7 feet tall and has a shallow, fibrous root system. Hardy in Zones 4–9.

Spotted Joe-pye Weed (*E. maculatum*) grows 3–7 feet tall and has purple spots on the stem, hence its common name. The EOL website notes that occasionally the stems may be all purple and are sometimes hairy. There are 4–5 large leaves on each whorl. The large flower clusters are flat topped, rather than domed. Monarchs and Swallowtails flit about these flowers gathering nectar. The cultivar 'Glenda' is about the same size as 'Gateway' but has larger flowers. Disease resistant, it is a good choice for a rain garden.

Hollow-Stemmed Joe-pye Weed (*E. fistulosum*) grows 3–11 feet tall. It requires a moist planting site and has 4–7 leaves in each whorl. The hollow stems are smooth, with no hair, and blue or powdery gray-green. 'Gateway' is a popular cultivar that matures at 5–6 feet. It is hardy in Zones 4–8 and can be used in a rain garden.

Eastern Joe-pye Weed (*E. dubium*) is found in eastern North America and grows 15 inches to 4 feet tall. It has fine purple spots on the stem and dull pink flowers. The dwarf cultivar 'Little Joe' comes from this species. 'Baby Joe' is only 24–30 inches tall and has deep rose flower clusters on dark stems. It is very handsome.

PLANTING REQUIREMENTS

Plant Joe-pye weed in moist, well-drained soil in full sun. It will accept some shade but has a tendency to flop. Cut last year's growth to the ground in spring. My plant was beginning to look like a Joe-pye on steroids, so after it began to grow, I cut it back nearly to the ground in late May. It resprouted and became more manageable, although it bloomed much later. If your area gets early frosts, you may not want to do this. I don't know if this treatment will work with all of the *Eutrochium* species, but unless you have only one specimen and fear to lose it, give it a try. Sometimes a drier site will also keep this huge native in check.

PROPAGATION
Divide young plants in early spring or plant seed. Will self-sow.

Willow-Leaved Sunflower (*Helianthus salicifolius*)
Zones 4–9
5–8 feet
Blooms: Fall
Yellow flowers
Deer resistant

The best attribute of this massive perennial is its thin, willowy leaves. From a distance, the impressive foliage reminds me of Amsonia foliage on triple-triple steroids—or of a huge clump of unusual grass. It just doesn't look like a regular perennial sunflower. Attractive to birds, butterflies, and bees, Helianthus species bloom reliably and make a real statement at the back of a border or in a wild space. Just be advised that these garden giants can become aggressive if growing conditions become too comfortable.

'First Light', a 4-foot-tall cultivar, was named the Plant of the Week by the *Columbus Dispatch* (Columbus, Ohio) in February 2012. Two even smaller cultivars (18-inch 'Table Mountain' and 12-inch 'Low Down') are also available and are likely better choices for the average home garden. However, nothing can match the spectacular foliage display of the species.

Maximilian Sunflower (*H. maximiliani*), 3–8 feet.
The yellow sunflowers rise high above the leaves, bringing the total height up to 10 feet or more. This huge prairie perennial can be very aggressive once established. It's fun to grow in a wild area but not recommended for a normal perennial garden. In rich soil it can grow 12 feet tall and take over the world! However, you can cut these to the ground in midsummer. The resulting shorter plant will still bloom but will send out its flowers later in the fall than usual.

Helianthus may be used as an ingredient in range seeding mixtures to provide a high-quality forage for livestock and food and cover for wildlife. Cultivars are being bred specifically for these grazing sites. The U.S. Department of Agriculture website (*plants.usda.gov/plantguide/doc/pg_hema2.docx*) reports that "the USDA NRCS Plant Materials Center has released Maximilian sunflower cultivars 'Aztec' and 'Prairie Gold' for conservation use" (p. 3). 'Prairie Gold' is cold tolerant and 'Aztec' needs more moisture.

PLANTING REQUIREMENTS

Plant in average, well-drained soil in full sun. Spreads rapidly once established.

PROPAGATION

Divide young plants in early spring, cut new shoots from parent plant, or sow ripe seeds in the fall. Will self-sow.

Ox-Eye Sunflower, aka False Sunflower (*Heliopsis helianthoides*)

Zones 3–9

3–5 ft

Blooms: Midsummer to fall

Yellow flowers with yellow centers

Drought tolerant

Rain garden

Ox-Eye Sunflower is also called False Sunflower. A clump-former, it spreads aggressively. Planted intermittently with Obedient Plant, it now completely covers the bottom of a Minnesota church filtration basin. Instead of cracked dry mud, parishioners appreciate a sea of varying sizes and shades of green until late summer when all burst into a medley of bright yellow and lavender-purple. The species is well suited to its task.

Home gardeners might be happier with one of the smaller, more compact cultivars. One exciting cultivar is Neil Diboll's 'Prairie Sunset' with its lovely brownish-mahogany markings softly brushed around the center of each delicious golden flower. 'Summer Sun', 'Venus', and 'Ballerina' all have large semidouble golden flowers, grow to 3 feet, and seldom need staking. 'Golden Plume' is slightly smaller. 'Summer Nights' boasts red stems and reddish foliage that complements the deep gold composite flowers accented with a mahogany eye. If you are searching for something really different, check out 'Loraine

Sunshine', which has variegated nearly white foliage with vivid green veins. Like it or not, this cultivar will create discussion.

PLANTING REQUIREMENTS

Heliopsis appreciates average, well-drained soil. It does best in full sun. Do not baby it. This is a prairie plant with deep roots and once established it can withstand drought as well as occasional inundation. Deadhead to extend the bloom and to curtail self-sowing.

PROPAGATION

Divide young plants in spring, transplant seedlings or plant ripened seeds in fall. This plant self-sows.

Silphium spp.

Zones 4–8

2–6 feet

Blooms: Fall

Yellow flowers

In *Sand County Almanac,* Aldo Leopold wrote, "For a few years my Silphium will try in vain to rise above the mowing machine, and then it will die. With it will die the prairie epoch."

Rough, massive Silphiums were familiar denizens of the tallgrass prairie. They are too large for most home gardens except at the very back. Or add just one for historical interest.

The yellow flowers of most Silphiums are called sunflowers although they are much smaller than the familiar ones of Kansas. Most bloom from July through September.

Rosinweed (*S. integrifolium*) is the smallest of the lot. It usually matures at 3–4 feet, although it can stretch to 6 feet. Broken stems of this huge plant yield a bitter tasting sticky sap that Native Americans and early settlers chewed like gum.

Compass Plant (*S. laciniatum*) grows up to 9 feet tall. Huge leaves follow the sun, pointing north and south like monster hands. Pioneers traveling through tall prairie grass sought out the Compass Plant to help get their bearings. It has 4–5-inch, yellow sunflowers that bloom from midsummer to fall. Compass Plant is recommended for a rain garden.

Cup Plant (*S. perfoliatum*) attracts small birds, butterflies, and insects to drink from the cup that is created where the perfoliate leaf clasps the sturdy, hairy stems. Hummingbirds get a dual treat by devouring the insects that visit these water-filled cups. This 4–10-foot-tall prairie giant has large, golden-yellow sunflowers that bloom in the fall.

Prairie Dock (*S. terebinthinaceum*) is another Silphium with golden-yellow sunflowers. The rough leaves of this 4–10-foot perennial grow in a rosette close to the ground. It gets its height from the tall flower stalks that can bolt high in the air in a day or two. Prairie Dock is one of the last of the Silphiums to bloom, continuing into the fall.

PLANTING REQUIREMENTS
Plant in average, well-drained soil in full sun. Give them tough love. Rich, loamy soil will cause excessive growth and floppy plants. These prairie plants sink massive roots deep in the ground so dividing mature plants or attempting to remove or relocate them once established can prove nearly impossible.

PROPAGATION
Take divisions from young plants in spring, or transplant young seedlings. Plant ripened seed in fall.

6.
Great Ground Covers
Take Care of Problem Areas

Ground covers are Nature's carpets that clothe soil in a variety of green array and make this flowering world all the brighter and more beautiful.

—Daniel Foley

Ground covers are special friends. Most of us have a variety of friends. Each has a distinct personality with character traits and idiosyncrasies that we may like or dislike depending on the timing or our frame of mind. Some are always there, others may move in and out of our circle. But whatever the characteristics, each friend is important to us.

In many ways, the plants in our gardens resemble our human friends. Consider the perennials. These are the bold, colorful friends that brighten your day and can always bring a smile. Shrubs may not be quite as outgoing but are steady and will not disappear when the going gets tough. They lack the innate flashiness of those happy-go-lucky perennials but are probably your "classy friends." Trees are those incredible friends you realize are above you in so many ways, yet stand tall and firm, ready to protect you in any crisis. Ferns calm and soothe your troubled spirit, bringing softness and serenity. Vines scramble to the heights to please, happily shielding you from unpleasantness as they climb. Grasses change through the seasons, sometimes small and

Dwarf Crested Iris

inconspicuous, at other times waving wildly, demanding attention. Sometimes they are just plain, usually unobtrusive green; some of them, given time, become bright and colorful. They may be changeable, but are pleasant to have around. It is good to have variety in our circle of friends. But one friend is missing in this analogy: the one who is never demanding, never asks for extra attention, yet is "always there for you." In the gardening world, that friend is a ground cover.

Ground covers perform many functions. We employ them to cover difficult locations subject to erosion. They quickly blanket the area under the drip line of a tree where neither grass nor anything else willingly grows. They scramble down hillsides, covering every rock, nook, and cranny as they descend. Ground covers do not fuss if the area is wild and teeming with wildlife. Nor are they unhappy if they are off by themselves, quietly doing their own thing, unheralded and unobserved. Some will thrive in wet sites while others readily withstand drought.

What constitutes a ground cover? Super-aggressive native perennials such as Bee Balm and Evening Primrose that are allowed to run may play the role of ground cover. Chapter 7 gives examples of three potential thugs in the fern category that can become appropriate ground cover in the right location. In chapter 9 you will find several rhizomatous grasses that will happily clothe a troublesome area, waving gracefully in the breeze and providing cover for birds and wildlife. Even vines can double as ground cover. Native Virginia Creeper is a good example. Allow it to climb trees, train it to drape over fences or climb up a wall. Or let it ramble on the ground to provide a colorful red carpet in the fall.

The last plant description in this chapter is Canada Anemone. Because of its aggressive nature, it is often called Canada Enemy. Yet it is beautiful and in the right place it absolutely sparkles.

Not all ground covers are super-aggressive. In fact some are civilized, even timid. Occasionally, for the sake of design, we decide to include a mass of a single plant in the perennial border but do not want this choice to take over the entire area. Its function is to complement individual specimens nearby. Several well-behaved ground covers, with direction and encouragement, can make a great statement in the perennial bed. A good example is the tiny Dwarf Crested Iris. Its sharply pointed leaves bring a unique texture and form to the garden. Another option might be Coralbells. Think of all the current colors available at the garden center. An endless array of leaf patterns, colors, and sizes in recent cultivars awaits you. Many of these originated from *Heuchera sanguinea*, our western native. Choose some of these beauties to put pizzazz into a quiet corner of the perennial bed. Or plant the unassuming native Alumroot (*H. richardsonii*). It quietly fills a small area with no muss or fuss, yet does not get out of control.

Ground covers are versatile and will grow vigorously under trees or shrubs, along foundations or fencelines, or as part of a garden design. Natives are available for nearly every possible need. Why resort to boring and overused Periwinkle, also called Myrtle (*Vinca minor, V. major*), Purple Wintercreeper (*Euonymus fortunei* 'Coloratus'), or English Ivy (*Hedera helix*). Those three exotics—what I call the Terrible Three—have escaped to the wild, causing innumerable problems by covering huge areas that were once home to a variety of native species. Besides, aren't you tired of seeing them used everywhere in public landscaping? I am.

When we lived in Indianapolis, I served on the landscaping committee at the newly built Indiana Historical Society headquarters. The landscape architect recommended the Terrible Three as preferred ground covers around the site. As an opinionated native plant enthusiast (and wife of the IHS director), I fussed. Then I explained why Bearberry (*Arctostaphylos uva-ursi*) would be a much better choice. Bearberry is a historically significant plant also known as Kinnikinnick. Native Americans smoked it and used it in their cooking. It is hardy in Zones 2–7, grows 2–10 inches tall, and has pretty pinkish white flowers in late spring. In midsummer, clusters of bright red berries appear, often persisting into winter. Its leaves change from glossy summertime green to shades of burgundy and red in fall and often remain on the plant until new leaves push them off in the spring. Bearberry is a larval host for Hoary Elfin, Brown Elfin, and Freija Fritillary butterflies. Hummingbirds seek out this plant. Visiting schoolchildren could learn about this historic Bearberry. How could the committee refuse? And so Bearberry was installed in front of the Indiana Historical Society under new native Redbud trees.

Many homeowners plant Japanese Pachysandra (*Pachysandra terminalis*) as a ground cover. and while it is not nearly as invasive as the Terrible Three, native Allegheny Spurge (*P. procumbens*) is a better alternative. It grew beautifully at our Indiana home and now the transplants we brought to Minnesota are also flourishing. It is slower growing than Japanese Pachysandra, but has prettier, sage-green scalloped leaves with occasional muted splotches. The large white bottlebrush flowers handily beat out the flowers of its Asian cousin. I propagate native Pachysandra by cutting through the rooted rhizomes, separating out new pieces and transplanting them. I have tried rooting stem cuttings in sand but find root division easier and more reliable. Allegheny Spurge remains evergreen below Zone 6, but goes dormant in northern zones, reappearing in spring. This deer resistant ground cover is worth acquiring.

Here are some of my favorite ground covers. Some are aggressive, others are more timid, but all are easy to grow and will do what you ask of them. And as always, if you cannot find these plants or want something else, go online and search. Ask at the local garden center. Check out any ground cover that appeals to you. Just try not to be tempted by the Terrible Three!

Suggested Ground Covers

Dwarf Crested Iris (*Iris cristata*)
Zones 3–8
4–7 inches
Blooms: Late spring
Lavender flowers
Deer resistant

Gardeners seldom think of iris as a ground cover. However, when it is content, Dwarf Crested Iris can quickly fill a small space with its short swordlike green leaves. Its beautiful little lavender and yellow iris flowers bloom in April and May when masses of dainty flowers are such a delight to the winter-weary gardener. Rhizomatous roots create a tight mat, and effectively demonstrate that iris can be a serviceable ground cover.

A number of cultivars are available. White flowering 'Tennessee White' is recommended by Plant Delights Nursery. For deep purple flowers, look for 'Abby's Violet'. True to its name, 'Powder Blue Giant' has the largest flower in soft powder blue. It is sturdy and easy to grow.

PLANTING REQUIREMENTS
For the best performance, plant in humus-rich, moist, well-drained soil in full sun. This little iris abhors alkaline, clay soil and will rot if the rhizomes stay too wet. Dry soil is a better option.

PROPAGATION

Most experts recommend dividing and replanting divisions in late summer or early fall, but I often do my iris dividing immediately after blooming so they have a chance to settle in. Either method works. Do not plant rhizomes too deep!

Creeping Moss Phlox (*Phlox subulata*)

Zones 3–8

3–6 inches

Blooms: late spring

Pink, blue, white flowers

Fine, needle-like leaves blanket a space, remaining evergreen for year-round interest. In spring, the green foliage erupts with masses of small phlox flowers. It is a good choice for a rock garden, spilling over a stone wall, planted near the sidewalk, or at the edge of a border garden. 'Red Wings' is a brilliant hot pink. For shades of purple and lavender, choose 'Emerald Blue' or 'Purple Beauty'. 'Candy Stripe' has a lavender-pink strip down the middle of each petal. Endless colors are available so just go to the local nursery in spring and pick your favorite.

PLANTING REQUIREMENTS

Supply adequate moisture until established. Prefers average to loamy, well-drained garden soil in full sun, although it will accept some shade. Can tolerate mild drought.

PROPAGATION

Root cuttings or plant seeds. Division in early spring is possible but not always successful.

Stonecrop Sedum (*Sedum* spp.)

Zones 4–8

2–8 inches

Blooms: late spring

White flowers

Sun/part shade

Sedum thrives in hot, dry planting sites and will run happily over walkways, multiply in a rock garden, drape over a stone wall, or scramble around stepping stones meandering through a native plant garden. It is not a fussbudget and can get along anywhere. Woods Sedum (*S. ternatum*) is an unassuming succulent with fat whorled leaves that are covered with starry white flowers in spring.

Savvy sedum gardeners enjoy the flat-topped clusters of yellow flowers that bloom in May and June on Broadleaf Stonecrop (*S. spathulifolium*). However, most also insist that the handsome silvery-white succulent rosettes edged in red are the true stars of the show. Several selections are available in this species including popular 'Cape Blanco', a fantastic little sedum that changes color throughout the season choosing shades of pewter, silver, gray, sage green, and even hints of red. For selections with more tints of red look for 'William Pascoe', 'Red Raver', or 'Aureum'.

PLANTING REQUIREMENTS
Sedum does best in well-drained soil, especially if it is slightly sandy. It dislikes continually wet clay soils and will rot if the drainage is not corrected. It prefers full sun, but will tolerate some shade. Ground-hugging sedums tolerate dryness but need adequate moisture during flowering season. Do not fertilize. Sedums thrive on neglect.

PROPAGATION
Divide rosettes and transplant. They root easily just by touching the soil.

Wild Strawberry (*Fragaria virginiana*)
Zones 3–8
4–6 inches
Blooms: late spring to early summer
White flowers
Sun/part shade
Deer resistant
Just like commercial strawberry plants, native Wild Strawberry sends out long runners that root and start new plants. It has fuzzy leaves and pure white five-petaled flowers that surround a cluster of airy filament-like yellow stamens. It grows 4–6 inches tall. After the flowers mature, the seeds develop into edible strawberries. The only difference is their small size, but what they lack in size they make up for in sweetness. Wild Strawberry is the larval host for the Grizzled Skipper and Gray Hairstreak butterflies. It is one of two parent plants for our commercial strawberries. The other is *F. chiloensis*.

It makes a pretty ground cover that will scramble loosely over the ground. And who doesn't want a ground cover that produces delicious fruit? But if you plan to enjoy them you will have to hurry, because those ripe strawberries are a treat for game birds, songbirds, and small mammals.

This cool-season plant grows well in spring and fall, but may go dormant in the heat of summer.

Barren Strawberry (*Waldsteinia fragarioides*)

Zones 4–8

3–6 inches

Blooms: late spring

Deer resistant

Rain garden

In spring Barren Strawberry is covered with lovely soft yellow flowers. After the flowers fade, the light green evergreen leaves create a dense, tight ground cover. Barren Strawberry produces dry strawberry-like fruits that provide an attractive glimpse of red under the leaves, but they only tempt. They are not edible. The ground-hugging foliage accepts light foot traffic. Avoid purchasing the Asian selection (*W. ternata*).

PLANTING REQUIREMENTS

Both species grow best in average to rich loamy, well-drained soil with some moisture in full or part sun. Barren Strawberry will tolerate clay soil.

PROPAGATION

Separate rosettes that have run from the mother plant and transplant them. Divide Barren Strawberry in late spring after blooming has stopped or in the fall. Keep watered in the heat of summer.

Coralbells (*Heuchera sanguinea*)

Zones 4–9

6–8 inches

Blooms: late spring to early summer

Sun/part sun

Deer resistant

Rain garden

Most gardeners are familiar with Coralbells and appreciate their ability to serve as a modest ground cover. *Heuchera sanguinea* is native to the western United States and has been used by hybridizers to create many new cultivars and hybrids including bright red 'Firefly', blood-red 'Ruby Bells', and scarlet 'Fairy Cups'. 'White Cloud' has white flowers and round, silvery mottled leaves. 'Apple Blossom' proudly displays a bicolored snowy white flower tipped with pink.

Alumroot (*H. richardsonii*) is a taller native Heuchera that was a regular resident of tallgrass prairies. Its tiny greenish flowers soar 2–3 feet above the hairy leaves and bloom in May to June. Mass this upright native for an effective ground cover, plant it in a rock garden, or include it in a native garden.

PLANTING REQUIREMENTS

Plant in loamy, humus-rich, well-drained soil. Provide moisture during the heat of summer. Drought tolerant once established.

PROPAGATION

Divide clumps in spring. The Missouri Botanical Garden website recommends division every three years to prevent the roots from becoming too woody.

Canada Anemone (*Anemone canadensis*)

Zones 2–7

12–18 inches

Blooms: summer

White flower

Sun/part sun

Rain garden

What a great ground cover! Canada Anemone does exactly what every gardener dreams of and thoroughly covers a bare space with lovely, deeply divided buttercup-like leaves. In a sunny spot, the entire patch will be dancing with a host of dainty white flowers boasting a bright yellow center.

Canada Anemone spreads through underground rhizomes or by windblown seed. And spread it will. So beware! Do NOT plant this pretty thing in your perennial bed or anywhere it cannot follow its dreams and run, run, run—unless you want eternal maintenance and intense frustration.

"Canada Enemy" can be a real thug. But plant it where it doesn't need restraint and it will be your friend forever.

PLANTING REQUIREMENTS
Plant in average, well-drained soil in full or part sun. The more sun it receives the more it will bloom. Take precautions if you plant this aggressive beauty, and make sure that you choose the site wisely. Don't say I didn't warn you!

PROPAGATION
Divisions taken in spring or fall transplant easily as long as you provide adequate moisture until they are well established. Self-sows, or plant seed. Seedlings will take up to three years to bloom.

Nature was surely in a gentle mood when she created the ferns.

—Henry and Rebecca Northern

7.
Fantastic
Ferns

Bring Softness into the Garden

Most gardeners assume that ferns require shade. True, most of them do. But sun-worshipping gardeners will be pleased to learn that several ferns grow well in sun. There is one overriding caveat: they all require a consistently moist planting site. Only then are they able to provide an airy, feathery texture to your sun garden.

On the popular website davesgarden.com, there is a 2008 article detailing ferns that can tolerate sun. In it Todd Boland, research horticulturist at the Memorial University of Newfoundland Botanical Garden, explains that ferns have had a rather checkered history. They were in high demand during the Victorian era, especially in the United Kingdom, and then became favored only by specialty gardeners. Thanks to colorful Asian Painted Fern availability, ferns are once again sought after. They are recommended as companion plants for hostas and have become a staple for the shade garden. Ferns are used as focal points, planted in a mass to create textural interest, employed as a ground cover, and incorporated in sunny perennial gardens.

Ostrich Fern

Cinnamon, Royal, and Interrupted ferns (*Osmunda* spp.) enjoy growing in the sun but they also all demand moisture. If the soil dries at all, this sunny trio will negatively wave their fronds at you, dry up, and go dormant. Keep them well hydrated into the fall and they will reward you with beautiful autumn hues of bronze and gold.

Lady and Male Ferns enjoy sunny locations but both insist on adequate libation. Lady Fern (*Athyrium felix-femina*) maintains a very ladylike presence in the garden. She is definitely not the running-around type but simply adds to her girth in a genteel, ever-increasing clump. Male Fern (*Dryopteris felix-mas*) sports leathery fronds. Unlike his deciduous lady friend, Male Fern retains his heavy green fronds, only shedding them when new ones emerge in the spring.

Some sources recommend Ostrich Fern (*Matteuccia struthiopteris*) as a fern to grow in the sun. In northern gardens it performs well in sunny, well-mulched locations, but in warmer zones it does not fare as well. In hot, humid zones it requires shady protection during the hottest part of the afternoon. Above all, keep this fern well watered. If it becomes the least bit dry, the fronds tatter, and even if the plant does not go dormant, you may wish it did.

In nature, ferns are usually found in moist, fertile spots with good drainage. For success with ferns, try to replicate their natural soil. Add organic material. Mulch heavily to retain moisture, but keep the mulch away from the crown. Some old gardening books recommend "planting" potato-sized rocks underground near the roots of any moisture-loving plant to help retain soil moisture. I tried it with shrubs and it seemed to help, so if you want to grow ferns in the sun, grab a few rocks to plant and give it a whirl.

Several little species such as Spleenwort and Hairy-lip Fern do well in rock gardens or tucked in crevices in stone or rock walls. These are listed in the plant descriptions below.

Some of the more aggressive ferns are great ground covers in wet, problem areas. I have included three of these. Be advised that these three potential thugs are not suitable for the border garden. If the border is moist, this trio will quickly take over. But they are "sissies" and if they cannot guzzle that necessary drink whenever they want, they will languish and dry up. So if you need to reestablish control, just cut off their drinks.

Most ferns prefer loamy, rich, well-drained soil; some will thrive in moist clay. Ferns originate from spores, rather than the usual seed. Cut damaged or broken fronds off at ground level. Often a new frond will sprout later in the season. All of the suggested ferns will tolerate sun. They are arranged in order of size and potential use in the landscape.

As you plan a native plant perennial garden or border, consider incorporating a few ferns near other moisture lovers. Choose the well-behaved clump formers rather than the aggressive, rhizomatous ones. Planning for easy maintenance is important.

Suggested Ferns

Maidenhair Spleenwort (*Asplenium trichomanes* L.)

Zones 3–9

3–6 inches

Rock garden

This pretty little miss resembles a miniature Maidenhair Fern. Tiny rounded leaflets march around small, fan-shaped fronds held above dark, wiry stems.

Ebony Spleenwort (*A. platyneuron*) is a slightly larger plant growing 8–20 inches tall. It resembles a miniature Christmas Fern with pointed leaflets.

Hairy-lip Fern (*Cheilanthes lanosa*)

This is another tiny (6–8 inch) fern to tuck into a rock wall, in a rock garden, or plant a small mass at the edge of a rain garden. It has small leaves covered with downy, rust-colored hairs. The roots will form dense mats if the location is to its liking. It needs sharp drainage and will rot in soil that is not well drained. It accepts periodic dry spells once established.

PLANTING REQUIREMENTS

Tuck humus-rich, moist soil into crevices in a rock wall and plant these little gems. Mist occasionally with a fine sprayer and keep the soil moist. Drought brings early dormancy, but don't worry. They will reemerge with the return of adequate moisture.

PROPAGATION

Gently divide in spring or fall.

Cinnamon Fern (*Osmunda cinnamomea*)

Zones 3–9

24–36 inches

Deer resistant

Rain garden

The Latin word *cinnamomea* means cinnamon or brown; the fertile fronds do resemble cinnamon sticks. Unlike the attractive brown fertile fronds of well-known Ostrich Fern, the mahogany-brown fronds of Cinnamon Fern collapse and disappear in midsummer after dropping their ripened spores. Hummingbirds collect the fuzz to line their tiny nests.

A clump former, slow-growing Cinnamon Fern lends its handsome, airy presence to any moist garden. The edible fiddleheads emerge very early in the spring. Ruffed Grouse, deer, and other critters enjoy nibbling this tasty treat, but they do not bother the plant once it has donned its summer foliage.

PLANTING REQUIREMENTS

Cinnamon Fern REQUIRES humus-rich, moist soil in sunny locations. It is not tolerant of drought or even occasional dryness and will die without a consistent supply of life-giving moisture.

PROPAGATION

Divide young plants in early spring or in late fall after they become dormant. The massive root systems of mature ferns may be difficult to divide.

Royal Fern (*Osmunda regalis*)

Zones 3–9

24–48 inches

Rain garden

Royal Fern grows like a small shrub with leaves that look more like Locust Tree leaflets than fern fronds. It requires consistent moisture to survive, especially in a sunny location. This regal fern is striking whether used as a single specimen, planted in a drift, or massed. It turns bright yellow in the fall.

This is a true moisture lover and will even grow in the middle of a stream. Needless to say, it does not enjoy drought. If you have a wet planting area, a small stream, or even a manmade pond, Royal Fern will be a delighted resident. It is possible to grow it at the bottom of a rain garden depression, but during periods with no rainfall a rain garden becomes a dry garden, so you may have to add a little water to keep your royalty content.

PLANTING REQUIREMENTS
Moist soil required. Do not let Royal Fern get dry—ever! It can tolerate clay soil.

PROPAGATION
Divide young plants in early spring or fall. Keep transplants consistently moist.

Aggressive Ferns for Ground Cover or Erosion Control

Sensitive Fern (*Onoclea sensibilis*)
Zones 2–9
2–4 feet
Ground cover
Deer resistant
Rain garden

The flat, broad fronds of Sensitive Fern do not resemble familiar ferns. The edges are light green and wavy rather than toothed. Once frost hits, this fern dies to the ground. Why? Because it is sensitive to cold, hence its name. Sensitive Fern is also called Bead Fern. Flower arrangers collect the stiff, upright, fertile fronds tipped with clusters of silvery-black beads. If left undisturbed on the plant, these long-lasting beads will persist throughout the winter and can even last a year or two. They create winter interest in the garden.

Sensitive Fern that is grown in sun requires a much wetter environment than in shade. It may stretch taller with more moisture.

PLANTING REQUIREMENTS
Plant in average, well-drained soil with consistent moisture.

PROPAGATION
Divide in early spring. The thick rootstalk runs underground. Cut through it between individual plants to transplant a "start" elsewhere. Keep the roots moist until the new plant is established.

Marsh Fern (*Thelypteris palustris* var. *pubescens*)
Zones 3–10
12–18 inches
Deer resistant
Ground cover
Marsh Fern is an attractive, rapidly spreading moisture lover that will blanket a wet spot where not much else will grow. It even tolerates standing water. Its botanical name describes it perfectly. *Thelypteris* means female fern and *palustris* means marshy or swampy, describing the preferred planting environment for this aggressive fern. So if you tromp through a marshy area and find a huge colony of ferns, guess what it might be?

New York Fern (*T. noveboracensis*) is slightly taller at 24 inches, but enjoys a similar planting environment. These tough, spreading ferns both enjoy growing in sunny spots as long as there is sufficient moisture. They will even tolerate some dryness once established.

Experts check the lower leaflets on these ferns as one means of identifying which is which. The lower leaflets of a New York frond become considerably smaller as they descend. Marsh Fern's lower leaflets stay about the same size as the ones above. An identifying feature of both of these ferns is a slight hairiness on the back of the central frond stalk (rachis).

William Cullina notes that because the fertile fronds emerge later than the sterile ones, gardeners need not be reluctant to mow this ground cover in late spring or early summer.

PLANTING REQUIREMENTS
New York Fern enjoys rich, slightly acidic soil. Marsh Fern becomes denser and more luxuriant when it grows in soil with less acidity.

PROPAGATION
Divide in early spring, separating the rhizomes and transplanting. Keep moist until established.

Hay-scented Fern (*Dennstaedtia punctilobula*)
Zones 3–8
12–30 inches
Deer resistant
Ground cover
Hay-Scented Fern makes a lovely, bright green, finely textured ground cover. It requires good moisture in sunny locations, but can be somewhat drought tolerant in shady spots. Fall changes the color of the triangular fronds to soft shades of yellow and gold. Cut or crushed fronds emit the delicate smell of new-mown hay, hence its name.

Deer dislike Hay-scented Fern. It is a good wildlife cover where it is allowed to grow without restriction.

PLANTING REQUIREMENTS
Plant in moist or even boggy soil. It will go dormant if it gets too dry.

PROPAGATION
Hay-scented Fern spreads from rhizomes. Cut through the rhizome to separate and transplant. Be sure to keep the soil moist.

8.
Vigorous Vines

Provide Height with Ease

Trumpet Creeper with Hummingbird

Then the Lord God provided a vine and made it grow over Jonah to give shade for his head to ease his discomfort, and Jonah was very happy about the vine.

—Jonah 4:6

It was February and I was delighted to be in Florida visiting our oldest son, Mark and his family near Fort Lauderdale. When Mark was a teenager in Indianapolis, he informed me emphatically, "When I grow up I am NOT going to have plants around my house. Only grass." Now that he *is* grown up, I am amazed at his landscaping prowess.

Minimal landscaping at his newly purchased home screamed for help, so Mark sketched a tentative plan that included a few tall trees, some flowering shrubs, space for perennials and annuals, but still left enough turf grass for our two little grandsons to tear around. Mark searched until he found just the right native palm trees for his front yard. Next, he researched Florida native plants to find a shrub that would do exactly what he needed for the privacy hedge at the back of the property. He also designed a small, attractive biohedge of natives at the corner of his patio to give color, texture, fragrance, and privacy. He even disguised the air conditioning unit and utility boxes with flowering native shrubs.

When I arrived, he hurried me outside to admire the results and talk about his next project. The unenclosed patio looked into neighbors' yards on three sides. No large trees cooled it during hot Florida afternoons. A newly planted shade tree would take too long to grow, so he decided to build a pergola over the patio, sinking 4×4 posts into the ground on three sides. It would be attached to the house on the fourth side. Slats across the top would buffer the sun's rays. My job as the "native plant mom" was to help brainstorm for what to plant.

The obvious choice for Mark's pergola was a fast growing, attractive vine. He wanted something evergreen or semi-evergreen, a vine with flowers to attract hummingbirds and butterflies. Gardeners can Google their particular state and find a website with a list of choices for a variety of plants. Our research for Florida native vines offered several possibilities.

Mark still has to build the pergola, but once that structure is in place he will visit local Florida nurseries to look for Trumpet Honeysuckle (*Lonicera sempervirens*) or Crossvine (*Bignonia capreolata*). During mild Florida winters the leaves remain evergreen, but when winter temperatures plummet below acceptable limits, semi-evergreen plants will lose their leaves. New leaves will emerge in spring. Both of these vines are also native in northern areas of the United States where they are deciduous. Trumpet Honeysuckle, also called Coral Honeysuckle, is hardy to Zone 4. It is a twining vine that attracts hummingbirds and butterflies to its nectar and songbirds to the bright red berries. Crossvine, hardy to Zone 5, is a fast-growing native that climbs by tendrils. Regardless of which one he chooses, Mark will include wire or string supports at the sides of the pergola for the vine to grab as it begins its climb. And when that fragrant vine finally scrambles over the pergola, just imagine sitting in its shade watching hummingbirds and butterflies within arm's reach.

How do vines climb?

When searching for a vine, the climbing method is probably the first information you need to know to make a good choice. You need a vine that is capable of climbing where you want. Vines climb in four different ways:

1. *Tendrils.* These vines send out modified leaves that become springy coiled tendrils. The tendrils grab onto anything they can encircle, including the branches of the vine itself. Vines with tendrils are good choices for a chain link fence, a wooden lattice, string, or wire mesh. They will not climb a wall or a tree. You may need to tie the young branches to attach the vine to the support

until the tendrils take over. Choose plastic coated tie-wraps, old pantyhose, or soft cloth strips that will not cut into the young vine as it begins its climb.

2. *Twining.* Some vines wrap their entire stems around whatever they touch. Their requirements are similar to vines with tendrils. A few, such as American Bittersweet, are fussy about the direction they twine. If the plant wants to twine in a clockwise direction and you start winding it counterclockwise, it will simply unwind and twine the way it wants. Avoid planting large twining vines too close to shrubs or small trees that might become overpowered. Encourage twining behavior by winding the vine around the support until it gets the idea and proceeds on its own.

3. *Aerial rootlets.* These vines exude a sticky cement to create holdfasts, clearly visible as rough brown areas wherever they attach. English Ivy is an example. Many college or university brick or stone buildings are clad in ivy; Ivy League schools take pride in their designation. Native Climbing Hydrangea uses holdfasts to race up tree trunks or hang onto the sides of boulders. Some vines use tendrils with small sticky suction discs at their tips to adhere to walls and flat surfaces.

Holdfasts can attach vines to walls, buildings, trees, and even slick surfaces such as plastic or glass. To start them off, stick some chewed gum on the surface and press the vine into the gum. Before long these vines will continue their ascent on their own.

Be aware that these aerial rootlets impact whatever surface they latch onto—sometimes negatively. Have you ever removed vines from a painted surface? Then you know there will be a lot of scraping and prep work prior to repainting. These vines, although good for keeping buildings cool in summer and warm in winter, can also sneak into cracks and crevices, between mortar, and even up under shingles. If you decide to plant a tenacious vine, you may want to install a frame that stands 4–6 inches away from the surface you want to cover.

4. *Thorns.* Climbing roses have thorns that grab onto whatever they touch, including the gardener! Attach rose canes to an arbor or a trellis or they will flop to the ground.

What kind of support do vines need?

Vigorous, aggressive vines can become so heavy they actually topple the structure they climb, so build strong. Pick an appropriate support to match the mature height of the vine. Clematis will grow happily on a 6-foot fan trellis or scramble up a pole enclosed with a tube of chicken wire. American Wisteria (*Wisteria frutescens*) is not a good choice for that fan trellis, but will grow nicely on an arbor or pergola, dangling beautiful flower clusters that can hang close enough to sniff. A Trumpet Vine will thrive on an arbor, a pergola, or a chain link fence as long as the structure will bear its weight. Dutchman's Pipe (*Aristolochia durior*), host plant for the Pipevine Swallowtail butterfly, might be an appropriate choice to cover the toolshed.

Hops (*Humulus lupulus* L.), native to North America, Europe, and Asia, is a larval host for the Red Admiral and Question Mark butterflies. This fast-growing perennial vine can add 10–20 inches a week and totally cover a wall in a single season. An Indiana friend with a gorgeous formal garden built a huge lattice fence across the north end of a large vegetable garden using hefty 4×4 timbers sunk into the ground. She planted hops, and before long garden visitors did not even notice the vegetable garden growing behind that huge "green wall." I always wondered how that free standing wall could stand without collapsing under the weight of the hops, but perhaps the 4×4s were sunk into concrete. I have never seen anything like it before or since, but it was effective.

How do I plant a vine?

Vines need rainfall so don't dig the planting hole under the overhang of the house or you will be forced to get out the hose. Vines require very little root space, but once they are planted soil amendment may be difficult, so it is wise to complete that task before planting. Dig a hole 8–10 inches deep and 18–20 inches wide. Amend the soil with enough compost and sand to build a loamy mix that drains effectively. Make a small mound at the base of the planting hole and spread the roots of the vine evenly over it. Replace just enough soil to hold the vine in place and then fill the hole with water. After the water drains away, continue filling the hole, tamp lightly, and water again. Mulch the newly planted vine and then water every 2–3 days for the first 3 weeks. Then water deeply once a week during the first growing season to be sure it is well established before the winter begins. Don't let it get dry. If you plant a vine in the fall, continue to water it until the ground freezes or until it is established.

Vines can be planted next to a building or sidewalk with no fear of damaging concrete. Flowering vines planted on a north, south, or west exposure will have more time to recover from early morning frost damage than those on the east side that get the first light of the morning.

Are there any vines to avoid?

Our oldest daughter tells about a school trip she took as a first grader. The teacher warned, "Do not eat those berries. They are poisonous." Soon the little boy who was often relegated to the "naughty spot" at school began sobbing loudly. "Oh, Mrs. Turner," he wailed. "I ate a berry. Am I going to die?" Temptation can be too strong to resist. Avoid planting vines with toxic berries where curious children might be tempted to take a taste.

Be able to identify Poison Ivy. "Leaflets three, let them be. Berries white, take flight," bears repetition. Also, "Hairy rope, don't be a dope," referring to the hairy looking aerial roots that climb up trees in the wild. In winter, this is all that remains of the plant aboveground.

Colorful, fluttering butterflies are fun to watch, but squeamish family members may not appreciate eating lunch under a vine-covered pergola with caterpillars crawling about. So if the vine you choose is a larval host plant, plant it a reasonable distance from the picnic table.

Why should I plant a vine?

Native vines demand small amounts of space yet add so much to the big picture. They give height and vertical dimension to places where that may be difficult to achieve. Imagine the color above and behind a perennial border. Camouflage an unsightly fence or building with an attractive vine. Stand-alone curved arbors say, "Welcome to my garden." A couple of seats within the vine-covered arch will allow you to enjoy fragrant coolness and frosty glasses of lemonade with a friend.

Suggested Vines

Trumpet Creeper (*Campsis radicans*)
Zones 4–9
Blooms: Summer
10–40 feet
AGGRESSIVE

John James Audubon got it right when he painted a hummingbird sipping nectar from a bright orange Trumpet Creeper flower. Gorgeous tubular flowers "pop" among the dark green leaves of this vine. Small creatures tuck into it as bees and butterflies flit above. My daughter covered a pergola with Trumpet Vine and quickly created a shady bower beneath. Kristen enjoys reading in this fragrant, enclosed space filled with pretty flowers and zinging hummers. Trumpet Vine climbs by aerial roots.

Trumpet Vine is also called Cow Itch because, in some people, it can cause an allergic reaction similar to a case of Poison Ivy. Dress accordingly and wear gloves when you prune this vine.

A word of caution for southern gardeners: this rambunctious vine is more difficult to control in your area than in the North. So Southerners may want to choose another option like Crossvine (described below) unless there is a site well away from buildings where it is free to roam. But even as with a recalcitrant, rebellious child, there are things to love about this plant.

Several better-behaved forms are available. 'Yellow Trumpet' (var. *flava*) is yellow; 'Red Sunset' is red with an orange throat; 'Praecox' is scarlet; 'Flamenco' is a beautiful salmon-red; and 'Apricot' is true to its name. Go online and look at the gorgeous red flowers of 'Stromboli'. Talk about zing!

Hybrids such as 'Madame Galen' and 'Indian Summer' result from a cross of Chinese Trumpet Vine (*C. grandiflora*) with American Trumpet Vine and are not true natives.

PLANTING REQUIREMENTS

Plant in average, well-drained garden soil and then neglect it. Pampering will only make it more aggressive. Gardeners often sink a large hefty pot in the ground to curtail the roots and I even saw a recommendation to include a saucer under the pot. And if the day comes when it is time to get rid of this handsome fellow, gardening blogs suggest using straight vinegar or water-softening salt dug in around the roots for a surefire kill. Just be advised that Trumpet Vine is not going to stay neatly in a border garden. Site it appropriately.

PROPAGATION

Divide runners in spring or fall and transplant. Collect ripened seeds from the tan capsules in fall and plant immediately. But this plant propagates adequately without your help.

Crossvine (*Bignonia capreolata*)

Zones (5) 6–9

15–40 feet

Blooms: Spring to early summer

Red, orange, salmon, and yellow flowers

Crossvine is an evergreen vine, similar to Trumpet Vine, but not nearly as aggressive. A hummingbird magnet, its dark green leaves complement the flared trumpet flowers in shades of red, yellow, and orange. Most flowers show off a vividly colored throat of a different color. 'Tangerine Beauty' has apricot-orange flowers with lemon-yellow throats.

If you are curious how this vine got its common name, just cut the stem to find what resembles a Greek cross inside. This vine uses tendrils to climb. At the ends of the tendrils are small suckering discs that allow it to hang on even tighter than vines using tendrils alone.

PLANTING REQUIREMENTS

Plant in full sun in average, well drained garden soil with sufficient moisture. This vine will tolerate some shade, but blooms best in full sun. Cut back 1/2 to 2/3 in spring to keep the vine in check. Mow or clip off runners.

PROPAGATION

Divide in spring or fall; plant ripened seeds in fall. Store in a container in the refrigerator humidrawer for 6 weeks to cold stratify for spring planting.

American Bittersweet (*Celastrus scandens*)

Zones 3–8

8–15 feet

Fall fruit

American Bittersweet is prized for its showy fruit. Gardeners and flower arrangers enjoy the vivid red pea-sized seeds tucked into flaring open orange jackets that cover this vine in the fall. The biggest challenge is making sure the vine is native and not Oriental Bittersweet (*C. orbiculatus*), an exotic that is becoming a pest in the wild. Here are a few identity checks: look for leaves that are oval, not round. The flowers and fruit of the native vine grow from the newest tips of the vine, not in the axils of the leaves. Pale yellowish insignificant flowers are another hint. Oriental Bittersweet's larger flower clusters are greenish-white.

American Bittersweet is dioecious; it requires both male and female plants to set fruit. It is hoped the nursery has its plants sexed accurately! Ask.

The stems twine around anything they touch, including each other. I love these twisted, gnarly stems in fall arrangements. The deer in my woods also love them and refused to stop nibbling them to the ground until I used a wire barrier. If bittersweet is not close to an upright to twine around, it will become a small shrub instead of a vine.

PLANTING REQUIREMENTS
Plant in average, well drained soil. American Bittersweet will grow in part shade, but for heavy fruiting, choose full sun.

PROPAGATION
Rub the pulp off the ripened seed and plant in fall. Cuttings also work, but it is easier to just plunk the seed into the ground. Cold stratification for 6 weeks in the refrigerator is necessary in warm climates.

Virgin's Bower (*Clematis virginiana*)
Zones 4–8
Blooms: Late summer
White flowers
12–20 feet
Sun/part sun
Panicles of dainty, white, four-sepaled flowers cover this pretty vine in July and August, and continue to bloom for about a month. In the center of each individual flower are long delicate filaments that change from silky green to brown as the seeds ripen. Because of this, Virgin's Bower is often called Old Man's Beard. It is not related to Fringetree (*Chionanthus virginicus*) with the same common name. Prairie Moon Nursery calls it "Prairie Smoke

on a Rope" because of its resemblance to early spring Prairie Smoke (*Geum triflorum*).

Virgin's Bower can be mistaken for the exotic Autumn Clematis (*C. ternifolia*) from Asia, but a discerning eye will note that the leaves are quite different. Autumn Clematis has smooth-edged leaves while the edges of Virgin's Bower leaves are jagged.

Another native clematis, Ground Virgin's Bower (*C. recta*) looks similar to the vine except that it scrambles along the ground instead. It can stand 3–4 feet tall. Cut the purple foliage of this fragrant plant to the ground in fall or in spring before new growth begins.

There are several hardy native clematis species available including Leather Flower (*C. viorna*), a delicate Zone 4–8 vine with lovely two-tone bell flowers and striking golden filament seedheads. Go online to find native clematis that will do well in your area.

PLANTING REQUIREMENTS
Virgin's Bower does well in average, well-drained garden soil that is occasionally moist. It can grow in sun or part sun, but the leaves will become chartreuse with more sun. It needs a support such as a wire or something narrow enough for it to twine around. Otherwise it will twine around itself and make a mess.

PROPAGATION
Self-sows readily. Transplant young seedlings or plant ripe seed in fall.

Vining Honeysuckle (*Lonicera* spp.)

Zones 4–9
Blooms: Early to midsummer
Orange, yellow flowers
15 feet
Deer resistant
The fused disc leaves of Grape Honeysuckle (*Lonicera reticulata*) are round and slightly cupped. Yellow flowers on short stems (or no stems) appear to be threaded through the center of each leaf. This native vine grows to 15 feet and blooms from late spring to early summer. When

the seeds ripen, a small cluster of juicy red berries sits on top of each cupped leaf. It climbs by twining its leaves and stems around whatever is at hand.

This particular species has a variety of names, both common and scientific. It is called Grape Honeysuckle, Yellow Vine Honeysuckle, and Moonvine. *L. reticulata* is the preferred scientific name although it is often referred to as *L. prolifera*. 'Kintzley's Ghost' was discovered and propagated by William "Ped" Kintzley at Iowa State University in the 1880s. Recently introduced into the horticultural trade, it develops circular silvery-white bracts that persist into fall. This unusual vine is resistant to aphids. 'Kintzley's Ghost' received the Plant Select Award in 2006.

Hummingbirds seek out long-blooming Trumpet Honeysuckle (*L. sempervirens*), probably the most popular native honeysuckle vine. It has bright orangey-red flowers that poke through the joined leaves, then clusters of bright red berries. In zones with mild winters, this vine can continue to produce flowers up until very late in the fall. In my Minnesota Zone 4, the flowers generally cease blooming in late summer and the red berries take over the show. It twines its woody stems about anything nearby and uses tendrils to climb. 'Cedar Lane' has deep red flowers. For coral flowers and mildew-resistant leaves, find 'Major Wheeler'. 'Sulphurea' is one of the best yellow flowering choices.

Yellow Honeysuckle *(L. flava)* is another desirable yellow-flowering native vine. This spring bloomer has yellow-orange flowers followed by handsome reddish-orange berries in fall. It is not invasive.

PLANTING REQUIREMENTS
Prefers average, moist, well-drained soil in full sun. Will grow in part sun or light shade, but full sun is necessary for the best blooms.

PROPAGATION
Rub the pulp off ripened seeds and plant in fall. Dig and transplant rooted seedlings in spring.

Virginia Creeper *(Parthenocissus quinquefolia)*
Zones 3–9
5–40 feet
Sun/part shade
Deer resistant

I consider Virginia Creeper a super-plant, because it serves equally well as a vine or a ground cover. Native plant gardeners either recommend it or really dislike it, but how can anyone say anything bad about something that provides food or cover for over 35 species of wildlife?

I kept trying to introduce Virginia Creeper to an ugly bridge support wall behind a native plant garden near the Indiana Historical Society in Indianapolis. Each time it would get any decent growth, it would disappear, obviously ripped unceremoniously from the wall. I finally observed the culprit. It was a city employee, directed to take care of weeds. I asked why he insisted on yanking down the vine and he retorted, "We don't want poison ivy growing here." After I explained the difference, the plant was allowed to grow. It covers the wall with beautiful leaves, climbing by tendrils and suckers.

Unlike the three-part leaves that scream "Poison Ivy!" the large palmate leaves of Virginia Creeper resemble a green-gloved hand. These five-part leaves turn red or yellow in fall. Poison Ivy has white berries; Virginia Creeper's berries are blue (and also toxic to humans). So even though these two vines resemble one another, there are readily identifiable distinctions.

The cultivar 'Red Wall'™ (*P. q.* 'Troki') has fire-engine red foliage, blue fruit, and only grows 18–30 inches. It is hardy in Zones 3–10. 'Star Showers'® 'Monham', a Proven Winners plant, sports leaves of almost white that are splashed and speckled with green. Fall brings shades of pink and red to these leaves.

Be aware that some people are allergic to the oxylate crystals contained in Virginia Creeper and can develop a wicked rash. Wear protective clothing when working with this vine.

PLANTING REQUIREMENTS

Plant in average, well-drained garden soil with occasional moisture in full sun or part shade. Fall color will be better with more sun. Virginia Creeper blooms on old wood so it can be pruned in midsummer after blooming ceases.

What a great place to enjoy a cup of coffee or a frosty glass of lemonade amidst bright flowering native perennials!

(*Above*) Airy clumps of tall Purple Moor Grass 'Skyracer' and native Little Bluestem provide vertical interest above multi-colored gravel, a soft evergreen "rug," and hefty rocks.

(*Opposite*) A beautiful hydrangea bush, Purple Coneflowers, Black-eyed Susan, sedum, and daylilies spill over tumbled chunks of rock.

(*Opposite*) As residents drive into their subdivision, they are greeted by a well-designed entry garden of flowering native perennials and shrubs.

(*Above*) Drought-tolerant Gaillardia marches along the edge of a border garden. The brightly colored red and yellow Blanket Flower attracts birds and butterflies.

Incorporating a small tree into the perennial border softens the corner of a house.

A variety of low ground covers is an effective accent along the edge of stone steps.

(*Above*) A tiny accent garden planted at the base of a tree or light pole can make the lawnmower's task easier.

(*Opposite*) Bright white daisies light up a rock retaining wall. Cranesbill Geranium, Bellflowers, and hostas fill ascending spaces.

(*Opposite*) Common Mullein with its yellow flowers and soft, woolly leaves is often mistaken for a native plant. This interloper probably sprouted here on its own, joining a group of natives on the hillside.

(*Above*) Fall brings welcome clusters of New England Asters to the perennial garden.

(*Opposite*) Blue Spruce branches create an effective backdrop for these congenial native perennials.

(*Above*) Sparkling with raindrops, the soft pink flowers of *Penstemon digitalis* 'Dark Towers' rise above deep burgundy leaves.

(*Opposite*) Masses of yellow-centered lavender asters stand tall in the middle of a fall perennial garden, but may need support at the back.

(*Above*) The brilliant red flowers of Bee Balm, also called Oswego Tea, bloom reliably in either full sun or part shade.

(*Above*) Purple Coneflower, a dependable perennial, is well known to gardeners. Hybridizers continue to create numerous cultivars for this familiar native that may be fun to grow. Experiment, but keep the species in your garden too.

(*Opposite*) A small Serviceberry clump tree brightens a fall garden. In spring, gardeners will be rewarded with white flowers followed by dark edible fruits.

(*Above*) Can you think of a more effective way to attract birds and butterflies to your yard than to plant colorful native perennials?

(*Opposite*) A sparkling stream flows through a rock-lined depression edged with a variety of grasses and ground cover.

Ox-Eye Sunflower opens its bright, daisy-like flowers in mid-summer and continues blooming until fall.

'Red Sprite' Winterberry Holly is heavily laden with bright red berries that persist into winter, even after the deciduous leaves fall.

A winter storm leaves this crabapple's persistent fruit encased in ice.

Hoarfrost coats the seedheads of Purple Coneflower left standing to tempt birds in the wintery garden.

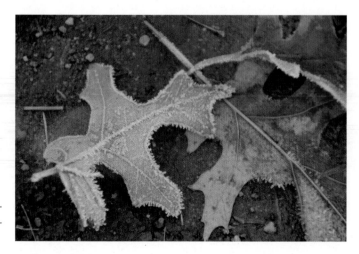

A Red Oak leaf coated with hoarfrost lies on an icy asphalt driveway.

Landscape design complements a house
and is important even in winter.

(*Right*) Liatris in shades of lavender and white rise above red flowering ground cover and a low growing evergreen to create an interesting corner garden on this homeowner's property.

(*Below*) A Red Wing, Minnesota, Master Gardener shows visitors the results of winter seeding in gallon milk jugs. Her lineup of planted containers is on the right. Each plastic jug is split, leaving the handle intact to create a mini greenhouse that is planted, spends the winter outdoors, and produces early seedlings for spring planting. What an easy way to get a head start on gardening!

A trio of River Birch trees and native grasses wear glittering coats of hoarfrost on a wintery morning.

The Redbud, a small understory tree, is one of the first flowering trees to signal spring.

Who is not fascinated by the wonders of native plants? This small child tries to count the minute seeds on a single flower growing in a field of Black-eyed Susan.

(*Above*) Tall red Cardinal Flower overlooks this quiet pond accented by large rocks. Whether a water interest is a rippling stream, a pond, a small sculpture (as seen on the opposite page), or even a simple birdbath, it is always a welcome addition to any garden, encouraging birds, butterflies and wildlife to visit often.

(*Opposite*) White candelabra-like spires of Cul-ver's Root create interesting vertical interest. This native perennial is especially effective when planted as a mass.

(*Above*) A huge boulder surrounded by upright grasses makes a statement near the edge of a large grassy area.

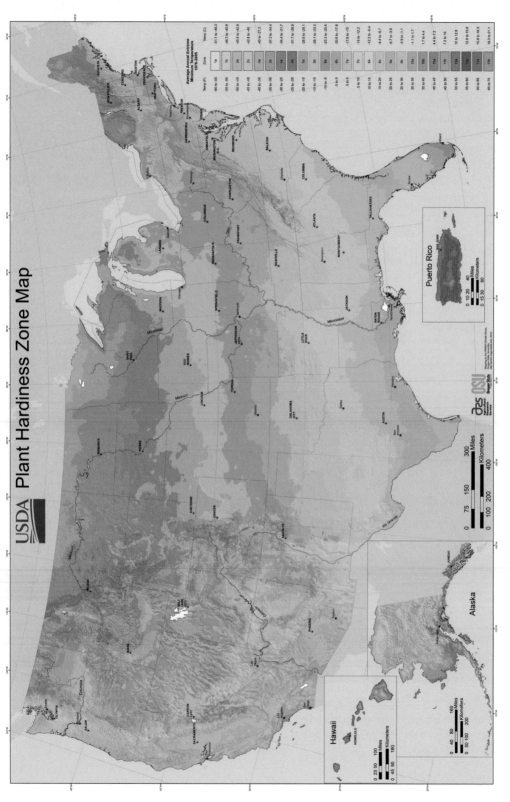

For an up-to-date, interactive version of this map with links to expanded maps for your state, go to plranthardiness.ars.usda.gov/PHZMWeb/#.

PROPAGATION

Clean ripened seeds to remove flesh and expose the small seeds within. Plant in fall, or cold stratify in the refrigerator for spring planting. Cuttings taken in spring will root.

Woodvamp *(Decumaria barbara)*

Zones 6–9

15–30 feet

White flowers

Blooms: Early summer

Sun/part sun

Woodvamp, often called Climbing Hydrangea, has 2–4 inch, flat-topped, white lacecap flower clusters. Butterflies enjoy the nectar and gardeners will love the soft fragrance. Because Woodvamp only flowers on new wood, gardeners need not hesitate to prune this vine in spring.

It has holdfasts so it can attach to a shed, a wall, or a tree as it climbs. It can also be trained on an arbor, a trellis or a fence. It will grow upright or scramble on the ground but only produces flowers when it climbs. In fall, this vine has pretty red berries.

Michael Dirr introduced a slightly smaller cultivar named 'Vickie' that is hardy in Zones 5–8.

PLANTING REQUIREMENTS

Prefers rich, slightlly acidic soil in a moist location. It does not tolerate drought. It will grow in a variety of light conditions.

PROPAGATION

Root softwood cuttings. Although this vine has tan seed capsules filled with many seeds, it takes many years for a seedling to reach blooming size.

American Wisteria *(Wisteria frutescens)*

Zones 5–9

20–30 feet

Deer resistant

American Wisteria produces 6–9 inch drooping panicles of lavender flowers which appear after the leaves emerge in late spring or early summer. Less aggressive, it is a much better choice than its Asian counterparts. Chinese *(W.*

sinese) and Japanese *(W. floribunda)* are considered invasive in parts of the United States. Our native American Wisteria also blooms in less than half the time it takes the Asian species to mature. It will cover arbors, pergolas, walls, or fences as long as there is sturdy adequate support. It climbs by twining, either clockwise or counter clockwise.

Butterflies seek out the nectar-rich flowers. American Wisteria is the larval host for skippers, Marine Blue and Duskywing butterflies.

Repeat bloomers include 'Amethyst Falls' which begins blooming more quickly than any other wisteria, occasionally after just a year or two. Its flowers are lavender. 'Clara Mack' and 'Nivea' both have white flowers. 'Longwood Purple' has deep purple flowers.

'Blue Moon' *(W. macrostachya)* is a Zone (3)4–9 selection of Kentucky Wisteria, bred to withstand Minnesota winters. This new cultivar is reportedly fully hardy to –40. It has fragrant blue flowers that bloom in early summer and rebloom throughout the season. I need to find a sturdy spot for this new beauty. Lighter pruning is recommended for 'Blue Moon'.

PLANTING REQUIREMENTS

Solid support is crucial for any wisteria vine. Plant in average, slightly acidic soil and provide adequate moisture, especially in the heat of summer. Site wisteria where it will have protection from early morning sunlight and possible frost damage. Buffeting winds may cause problems. Because this vine blooms on new wood, prune to 4–6 buds in late winter or early spring before new growth begins. It is possible to encourage a second flowering later in the summer by minimal pruning immediately after flowering, cutting just behind the faded flowers. Only fertilize lightly in early spring. Too much nitrogen will encourage lush leaf growth at the expense of flower production.

PROPAGATION

Root softwood or hardwood cuttings. Seed takes too long to develop into a flowering vine. Purchase hybrids and cultivars.

Of all the world's flowering plants, the grasses are undoubtedly the most important to man.

—R. W. Pohl

9.
Graceful
Grasses

Listen to Them Sing

Grasses are the mainstay of our native tallgrass prairies, which once covered 170 million acres beginning at the Indiana/Illinois border where natural woodlands gradually melded into vast native grasslands. They stretched from eastern Illinois to the foothills of the Rocky Mountains and covered land from the northern border of our country just below Saskatchewan all the way south to Texas. Iowa had the largest unbroken stretch of prairie, covering over 30 million acres. Only small remnants of this incredible ecosystem have survived. Yet rich deep soil still exists in testament to the deep roots and humus of those incredible grasses.

Early travelers referred to the prairies as "a sea of grass" where myriads of flowers in all colors of the rainbow bloomed. Pioneer diarists crossing the plains in their covered wagons extolled the glories of the seasons. Now only about 4 percent of our industrialized nation consists of native prairies, most of those restored remnants here and there. Yet recent sources still list over 800 species of non-woody flowering plants existing in these areas. Imagine how many more have been lost through development.

Prairie Cordgrass

In 1996, Congress set aside an 11,000-acre tract in the Kansas Flint Hills where, according to the National Park Service website, "the tallgrass prairie takes its last stand." NPS cooperates with The Nature Conservancy to manage this large prairie preserve. The Midewin National Tallgrass Prairie, near Elwood, Illinois, became the first federally designated tallgrass prairie the same year. As of January 2010 the site contains 18,225 acres and is administered by the U.S. Forest Service and the Illinois Department of Natural Resources.

Several books detail the demise of our prairielands, as did a one-hour TV documentary first aired in May 2001. Several youtube videos from this documentary are worth viewing. For starters, check out this excerpt hosted by Lyle Lovett: *Last Stand of the Tallgrass Prairies,* http://www.youtube.com /watch?v=jy21uSG3ma8.

A few decades ago, it was not fashionable to include ornamental grasses in landscaping projects and certainly not in formal gardens. They were acceptable in wild areas, but not in a suburban yard. Now they are a mainstay in perennial beds, along median strips, and in public spaces. They continue to increase in popularity as a welcome addition to the home landscape, providing a texture and sound like no other. It is hard to explain how the soft soughing and sighing of a mass of grass can affect your mood, but it does. It is unnecessary to plant a whole meadow to get the effect.

But I only have a small yard.

A nearby neighbor planted three large clumps of Indian grass in the center of a small garden at the edge of his front yard. He tucked clumps of Black-eyed Susan around the stately grass and edged the entire garden with 'Autumn Joy' sedum. It makes a strong statement at the point of his corner lot, but does not overwhelm. Another friend planted clumps of red 'Prairie Fire' Switch Grass at the end of a perennial border in front of her house. I saw Little Bluestem growing along the rim of a public filtration basin. In fall a sea of red surrounds that deep floriferous depression.

My Indianapolis DNR friend Lee Casebere plants masses of Prairie Dropseed along the walkway between the house and driveway. As Lee and his wife, Pat, walk to their car they often grab the fragrant seedheads just to enjoy the tantalizing scent they exude.

One of the first native grasses I became familiar with was Indiana friend Bill Brink's large clump of Sweetgrass, also called Vanilla Grass or Holy Grass

(*Hierochloe odorata*), growing in a corner of his perennial border. He told me that Native Americans considered it a sacred plant and called it "the hair of Mother Earth." Rub your fingers over a long arching leaf, bruising it slightly, to appreciate why this grass got its name. Native Americans braided Sweetgrass, let the braids dry, and then burned them as a smudge during prayer or purifying ceremonies. They also wove baskets from the leaves or brewed a tea to soothe sore throats.

Do grasses have any specific requirements?

When I first began growing grasses in my garden, I learned the hard way that it is necessary to cut them back to the ground in late winter before new growth begins. Otherwise it is nearly impossible to thin out last year's dead leaves.

Burning is the preferred way to remove dried growth from large prairies. We had a small garden just behind our house in Indianapolis where there was one huge clump of Big Bluestem. I decided upon burning as an easy way to get rid of the debris with an added bonus of warming the soil and encouraging faster spring growth. I had observed a spring burn at the Butler University campus prairie, so I knew that tall grasses could flare pretty high. But being a novice, I wasn't too worried. I cut my dried grass down by about half and touched it with a match. Yikes! The flames shot 15–20 feet in the air, the surrounding turfgrass began to burn, and I panicked. Fortunately the hose was nearby so I doused the fire quickly and that was the end of my pyromania. Now I just take hedge clippers to the big grasses and a scissors to the small ones and cut them off at ground level before spring growth begins. Friends who have large grass areas set the mower at 6 inches and mow the entire area before spring growth begins. Others use a weed whip.

How can I use grass in my home landscape?

Ground cover and erosion control are the most obvious uses. Clumps of some grasses can serve as focal points. Others will work as privacy barriers and double as mini refuges for wildlife.

Using native grasses or sedges as an alternative to turfgrass is becoming popular, especially in back yards, where design is more casual. I recently read about trials using Seashore Bentgrass (*Agrostis pallens*) sod in California. It is native to the Far West and is reportedly hardy to Zone 4. I am fascinated by the idea. To explore replacing part of your water-guzzling turfgrass with a more environmentally friendly alternative, look to recent books and websites. Contact native plant nurseries such as Prairie Nursery or Prairie Moon for suggested seed mixes. Check sources in your own state. The local extension agent may have suggestions.

However, to be honest, I have to admit my solution has been simple. I decrease the amount of turfgrass by adding more gardens and trying out one native plant after another. Elizabeth Lawrence got it right when she said, "As I grow older the days seem to get shorter—also the garden gets fuller." How true!

What grasses can I grow?

Below are some of the most familiar grasses of the tall- and shortgrass prairies. Each of these warm-season grasses can be grown in the home garden, although familiar Big Bluestem may have to be relegated to a special place to show off its size. Innumerable cultivars and hybrids showcase smaller, more compact sizes and vibrant color.

Include a few of these graceful, carefree natives in your garden. Grasses have so much history, and they are beautiful.

Suggested Grasses

Prairie Dropseed (*Sporobolus heterolepis*)
Zones 3–9
12–24 inches
Drought tolerant
Deer resistant
Rain garden

Imagine a small clump of fine-leaved arching grass at the edge of the garden. Grasp the tall seed stalks when they appear in midsummer and what do you smell? Popcorn! Graceful Prairie Dropseed is undemanding, easy to grow, and provides a fountainlike edging to any border. Or use this slow-growing native as a focal point at a curve in the garden where it is necessary to slow down and smell . . . the popcorn! It becomes a handsome golden-yellow accent in the fall.

PLANTING REQUIREMENTS

Plant in average, well-drained garden soil in full sun. It enjoys moisture, especially in the spring, but accepts dry conditions. Cut dried grass to the ground in spring before new growth begins.

PROPAGATION

Divide and transplant this warm-season grass in spring so it has plenty of time to adjust to being divided and transplanted before winter winds howl. Collect ripened seed and plant immediately or cold stratify to plant in the spring. Prairie Dropseed does not readily self-sow.

Sideoats Grama (*Bouteloua curtipendula*)

Zones 3–9

18–30 inches

Deer resistant

Rain garden

This interesting "one-sided" grass grows its flowers and seeds on only one side of the stalk. Plant gray-green Side-oats Grama near a sidewalk, next to steps, or at the front of the garden so you can appreciate its unusual behavior close up. It is intimidated by tall grasses or perennials and performs best when planted close to other "shorties." If the site is quite moist it can become aggressive, so utilize it as a ground cover in damp sites. It is pretty in the fall when the reddish seeds turn light tan and the leaves change to attractive tones of red, orange, and bronze. It is a larval or nectar source for a number of butterflies and skippers.

Blue Grama (*B. gracilis*) is often called mosquito grass because the tiny brush-like seedheads resemble insects buzzing above the dwarf-sized foliage. The leaves seldom rise higher than 8–12 inches. Like Prairie Dropseed, it deserves a planting site where its uniqueness can be readily observed.

PLANTING REQUIREMENTS

Plant in lean soil that is well drained and not consistently moist unless you want a good tough ground cover. Then provide more moisture. Cut to the ground in late winter or early spring before growth begins.

PROPAGATION
Divide clumps of this warm-season grass in spring. Plant ripened seeds in fall.

Little Bluestem (*Schizachyrium scoparium*)

Zones 3–9
18–24 inches
Deer resistant
Rain garden

The species is one of my favorite native grasses in the fall. Its brilliant red leaves literally glow in my garden in the sun and always get rave reviews from passersby. Little Bluestem is a clump-forming warm-season grass. It has small fluffy seedheads. 'Blue Heaven', a cultivar bred by Dr. Mary Meyer (University of Minnesota), stands 26 inches tall. Its bluish-green leaves change to show-stopping orange and reddish-purple in fall. This cultivar seldom flops. Zone 4 cultivars include 'Blaze', with vivid red fall color, and 'The Blues' (blue-green changing to burgundy-red in fall).

PLANTING REQUIREMENTS
Plant this dependable beauty in average, well-drained garden soil. Do not fertilize. It tolerates drought and thrives on neglect.

PROPAGATION
Divide in spring or sow ripened seeds in fall. It does not spread aggressively, nor is it a rampant self-sower. Cut to the ground before new spring growth begins.

Big Bluestem (*Andropogon gerardii*)

5–8 feet
Zones 3–9
Deer resistant
Rain garden
Turkey-foot seedheads wave high above this familiar drought-resistant native grass. The lush blue-green foliage turns red-orange in the fall. However,

the seedheads do not hold up as well in winter as those of some of the other native grasses.

This huge grass will bring historical dimension to your garden. Just remember why it is called *Big* Bluestem.

PLANTING REQUIREMENTS

Plant this deep-rooted warm-season prairie grass where it can stay. Once established it is difficult to move or divide. It is happiest in lean soil. Humus-rich, overly moist soil will make it flop.

PROPAGATION

Divide young plants in spring, transplant self-sown seedlings, or sow seed in fall.

Indian Grass (*Sorghastrum nutans*)

Zones 2–9

3–8 feet

Deer resistant

Rain garden

Indian Grass remains small and relatively insignificant for much of the summer. Then it suddenly perks up and sends up beautiful golden-bronze seedheads that stand straight and tall above the grass. It remains upright and handsome throughout the winter and is a good alternative to some of the popular exotic grasses. Attractive foliage in gold and yellow tones creates a nice accent in the autumn landscape. Birds and small mammals feast on the seeds, and skippers and butterflies enjoy the nectar from the ripening seeds.

'Sioux Blue' is one of the best cultivars. This sturdy upright grass has striking metallic blue summer foliage that becomes yellow-gold in fall.

PLANTING REQUIREMENTS

Plant in average garden soil with good drainage. Humus-rich soil and too much moisture can cause this beauty to sulk and flop over. It dislikes shade.

PROPAGATION

Divide young plants in spring. Mature plants are very deep-rooted and difficult to transplant or divide. Plant seed in fall or spring or transplant young self-sown seedlings.

Switch Grass (*Panicum virgatum*)
Zones 4–9
3–6 feet
Deer resistant
Rain garden

Graceful, airy Switch Grass has always been one of my favorite native grasses. I just wish it didn't self-sow so exuberantly! In a formal border, such behavior is not welcomed. In addition, cultivars seldom breed true, so those seedlings must be culled out. If you take the time to cut off the seedheads in fall before the seeds ripen and drop, that helps—a bit. However, delicate seedheads are still attractive during late fall and winter so that can create a dilemma for a tidy gardener. You must accept major hand weeding in spring if this grass is one of your favorites too.

For a brilliant red fall color in the garden, look for 'Rotstrahlbusch'. It is stunning. 'Heavy Metal' is slightly shorter with beautiful metallic blue foliage that changes to yellow in the fall. A cross of these two grasses produced 'Prairie Fire' with blue-green foliage that turns deep wine red. 'Shenandoah' leaf tips are red in midsummer and then change to all burgundy in fall.

PLANTING REQUIREMENTS
Switch Grass likes a little moisture in the soil and will thrive in difficult planting sites. I planted it at the bottom of a filtration basin that has intermittent periods of flooding and absolute drought. The Switch Grass waves gaily through it all.

PROPAGATION
Divide in spring or sow ripened seeds in fall. Self-sows readily.

Aggressive grasses for erosion control

Prairie Brome (*Bromus kalmii*)
Zones 3–6
20–30 inches
Sun/part sun
Erosion control
Deer resistant

Prairie Brome, also known as Kalm's Brome, seldom tops 2 feet. The heavy drooping seedheads resemble oats waving gracefully in the breeze. Plant this pretty bluish-green grass where it is free to run. It controls erosion even on steep slopes. It is found in wild moist areas with Bluejoint Grass and Joe-pye Weed. It can be short-lived but reseeds freely, so once established it is probably there to stay.

PLANTING REQUIREMENTS
Prairie Brome will grow in average soil, clay, or gritty sand. It likes average moisture, and, once established, does fine in drier sites. It is useful as erosion control, as a planting over a septic system, or as a grassy ground cover in a sunny spot.

PROPAGATION
Divide in spring or plant ripened seed.

Bluejoint Grass (*Calamagrostis canadensis*)
Zones 3–9
3–5 feet
Shoreline restoration
Sun/part shade
Deer resistant

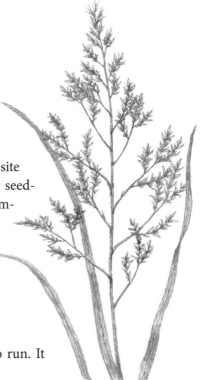

If you are looking for a clump-forming grass with at-tractive seedheads that stands up well in the winter, can quickly cover an area prone to erosion, and your planting site is moist or even wet, then this is your choice. Nodding seed-heads exhibit tones of gold, bronze, and purple in midsummer, fading to tan as the season progresses. In fall, the foliage can change to deep red. Often used in wetland restoration, Bluejoint Grass is too aggressive for a border garden, but choose the right spot and it will per-form its job admirably.

PLANTING REQUIREMENTS
Plant in moist or wet soil and give it plenty of room to run. It spreads by runners and will make tight mats to hold soil.

PROPAGATION
Separate rhizomes. This species self-sows prolifically and needs no assistance.

Purple Lovegrass (*Eragrostis spectabilis*)

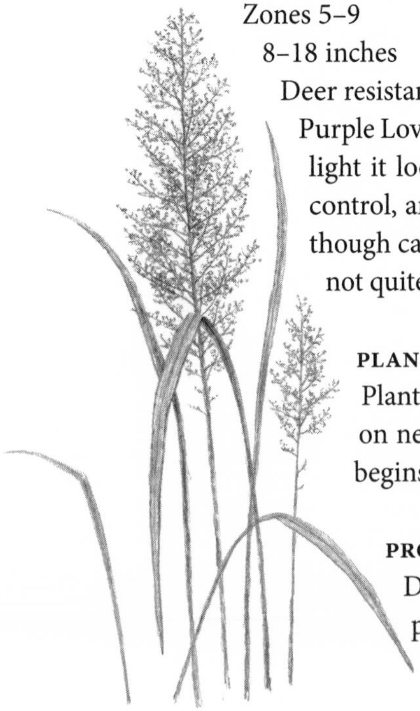

Zones 5–9

8–18 inches

Deer resistant

Purple Lovegrass creates a soft, low, pale lavender-rose haze. In certain light it looks almost red. It is a pretty ground cover, offers erosion control, and can even be used sparingly in a native plant garden, although care must be taken to keep it in bounds. If kept fairly dry it is not quite so rambunctious, but it is happiest when allowed to run.

PLANTING REQUIREMENTS
Plant in lean, well-drained soil. This is another plant that thrives on neglect. Cut foliage to the ground before new spring growth begins.

PROPAGATION
Divide rhizomes in spring, transplant self-sown seedlings, or plant seed in the fall.

When you plant a rain garden in your yard, you mimic some of the benefits of the natural landscape.

—Rusty Schmidt

10. Rain Gardens

Cleansing Storm Water with Native Plants

In a Minnesota Public Radio segment on rain gardens, Stephanie Hemphill noted that a good midwestern summer storm can dump a lot of water in one place, occasionally flooding into sewer lines or even spewing untreated sewage into lakes and rivers. She added, "Cities across the country are spending millions of dollars to solve the problem."

Especially in urban settings, sunny rain gardens featuring civilized native plants solve problems and make strong statements. Properly engineered and planted, these gardens can be striking, channel roof and driveway runoff to good use, reduce chemical applications and mowing, and break up the monotony of turf landscapes. Progressive municipal governments bent on reducing surges of water and chemicals in storm sewers may offer expertise and even dollars for carrying out your plan. In times of tension between citizens and government, a community of interest is refreshing.

Indeed, citizen by citizen, we can contribute to the public good. The "nature of nature" is such that no two environments are exactly alike. Therefore my experiences

Rain garden drawing

with sunny rain gardens are not directly applicable to your situation. Yet the principles are similar. To make my points I shall refer to three of my experiences. The first involves my own property and two others are at my church, a small congregation that underwent an expansion program.

It's a fact: in the northern United States, a concrete driveway IS cracked or WILL crack. With the annual frost heave, there is little to prevent this phenomenon. Our concrete driveway was no exception. The cracks that were evident in 2003 when we bought this 10-year old house had worsened and in the spring of 2011, the driveway had actually sunk a little below the level of the garage floor. Time for a change! We chose pavers, reasoning these would move without the disastrous consequences movement brings to concrete and asphalt driveways. Rain could also soak between the pavers, but one more dilemma involved the front sidewalk. Rain from the roof poured from the downspout and tore across the walkway and down the driveway. The persistent winter ice-skating rink was neither welcome nor safe. What was the solution?

The answer came when I signed up for Dakota County's Blue Thumb Rain Garden classes, advertised to teach homeowners how to help the environment by planting a garden. Using slides and lectures, Mike Isensee and Curt Coudren of the Dakota County Soil and Water Conservation District explained that storm water, when directed to a garden filled with deep-rooted perennials, soaks into the ground slowly. Because soil and plants remove pollutants, water leaving a rain garden is much cleaner than if it runs straight to the street.

Look around your neighborhood. Most home gardens are flat or mounded in the center. Conversely, a rain garden is a shallow depression that collects storm water from the roof, driveway, or sidewalk. Goals of rain gardens differ from those of a wetland or an ornamental pond. Rain gardens should totally drain within 24–48 hours and be dry more often than wet. Consequently, breeding mosquitoes are not an issue. Our instructors guided us through the following steps:

How to begin?

1. Choose a site in full sun and at least 10 feet from the foundation of a home. Never place a rain garden over the drain fields of septic systems, over utility lines, or within a troublesome wet spot. Lawns generally slope away from the foundation of a house to avoid creating a wet basement. An ideal rain

garden location should slope 4–12 percent. If the slope is 4 percent or less, guidelines recommend digging the rain garden 3–5 inches deep. If it is between 5 and 7 percent, dig it 6–7 inches deep, and for those slopes between 8 and 12 percent it should be about 8 inches deep. Slopes over 12 percent, are too steep so you will need to find another spot.

2. To determine how effectively water drains from a chosen location, dig a straight-sided hole 6–8 inches deep and fill it with water. If the water does not drain out within 24 hours, find a different location.

3. After determining the best location, mark the size and shape of the proposed rain garden with a hose, rope, or heavy string.

4. Spray-paint the outline if you are not planning to dig immediately.

5. Cut around the outline with a spade and remove the sod.

6. The bottom of the rain garden should be no deeper than 4–8 inches. To determine the proper depth of your chosen space:

   a. Drive in a stake at the top (uphill) of the proposed garden.

   b. Tie a string to that stake at ground level.

   c. Pound in another stake on the bottom (downhill) side of the garden.

   d. Pull the string taut between the stakes and tie it securely. Use a carpenter's level to ensure the string is horizontal (resembling a tightrope).

   e. Measure the distance from the string on the downhill stake to the ground.

   f. Measure the length of the string.

   g. Divide the height (e) by the distance (f). Multiply the result by 100 to determine the percentage of drop.

7. Slope the sides to the bottom of the depression. The bottom of the depression must be flat. Use a carpenter's level or a board to get it as level as possible.

8. Collected rainwater should remain in the depression until it soaks into the ground. To ensure that water from a heavy storm will not fill the depression too quickly and overrun the sides, use the soil you removed to build a small berm across the downhill edge and continue it up both sides, tapering as you approach the top. Leave the upper side open to allow runoff to enter the depression. Pack the soil of the berm firmly to prevent erosion.

9. Edging around the rain garden will give it a finished look and prevent weeds and grass from creeping into the garden or the berm.

At the conclusion of our class, we each received *The Blue Thumb Guide to Raingardens,* a sheet of graph paper, two stakes, a length of heavy white string and a plastic 4-inch carpenter's level with its traditional bubble.

I chose to install a rain garden near the troublesome downspout, so I checked the drainage first. Next, I marked off the garden shape, set the stakes, connected them with string, and tied it taut. The string on my downhill stake was 10 inches above ground level. The length of the string between the two stakes was 12 feet (144 inches). 10 divided by 144 equals .0694. Multiply .0694 times 100; that equals 6.94. According to the instructions, my proposed area had a drop between 5 and 7 percent, so I dug it 6–7 inches deep. Perfect. I did not need to make any further adjustments to achieve the right slope. You may have to.

Before long, the contractor came to begin construction work on our new paver driveway and walkway. We explained the rain garden concept and he agreed to work with us. First, his workman dug a depression with a small Bobcat. Next he buried a black plastic catch basin below the downspout next to the house and attached a white 6-inch rigid PVC pipe to its outlet. He laid the pipe a few inches under the proposed sidewalk area, guided it down the slight slope, and terminated it in the center of the bottom of the new rain garden. He attached the end of the pipe to a U-joint with a simple pop-up drain that sits on the surface of the ground. The underground pipe channels the roof runoff under the sidewalk and into the rain garden. This straightforward solution to our drainage and ice concerns employs no high-tech devices to cause future problems.

I used the soil the contractor removed to shape berms at the downhill edges of the garden and created gently sloping sides to the bottom. Next, I mixed a small amount of compost into the original soil, leveled the bottom of the depression, installed the plants, and spread 2–3 inches of shredded hardwood mulch over it all.

Plants on the lowest part of my rain garden enjoy moist soil and will tolerate occasional flooding. Those on the sides thrive in average gardening sites, and plants on the berms do best with drier conditions. These are the plants that can tolerate occasional drought. Our rain garden measures approximately 20 feet wide and 36 feet long. It is small but effective, catching much of the runoff from our roof, stopping and filtering it. No longer does our storm water tear downhill to the street and pour into the storm grating in the gutter.

Can other types of gardens handle storm water?

Certainly. When Heritage Lutheran Church in Apple Valley, MN built its new addition in 2009, the city insisted that the contractor add two deep filtration basins to collect runoff from the extensive roofs and parking areas. The church is located with a busy street on one border and a small lake on the other. I was not excited about the city's recommendation to seed the filtration basins with Minnesota DOT's Roadside Grass Mixture #210 but hit a brick wall with the church building committee when I suggested planting the basins with a mixture of native trees, shrubs, and perennials. I argued that these plants would not only beautify the church property, but could help with drainage and erosion problems inherent in these mandated basins. I eventually prevailed and with help and direction of my Blue Thumb instructor, Mike Isensee, our filtration basins are slowly but surely developing into attractive areas.

Mike recommended purple Obedient Plant for the bottom of the basin near the street. This disobedient dude naturally runs and reseeds at will, and it is perfect for achieving a total cover-up in the bottom of the basin. Bright yellow Ox-Eye Sunflower provides a good color contrast. Switch Grass tolerates occasional inundation as do a few native willow shrubs. We planted two River Birch clumps. On the sides are Snowberry bushes, a multitude of sun-loving prairie perennials that bloom throughout the growing season, and grasses that prefer slightly drier, well-drained planting sites. Dwarf Bush-Honeysuckle and 'Gro-low' Sumac provide erosion control, and Red Twig Dogwoods supply winter color. Mike recommended massing Little Bluestem around the top of that basin.

The other filtration basin is located near the lake and looks more like a wildflower meadow than the more orderly front basin. In it we planted Swamp Milkweed, Turtlehead, Joe-pye Weed, Sneezeweed, Ox-Eye Sunflower, Bee Balm, Black-eyed Susan, Great Blue Lobelia, Cardinal Flower, Liatris, Indian Grass, and Switch Grass.

City officials and Heritage members are pleased with the operation and appearance of our filtration basins. Both have seasonal color and interesting flowers and foliage; best of all, both drain properly within the city's stringent guidelines. No runoff from Heritage property flows into Apple Valley's storm sewer system.

My third experience with a rain garden involved an enclosed courtyard at Heritage. We needed to slow roof runoff and camouflage a large domed drainage grate. I purchased and hung a rain chain from the eaves trough. It prevents splattering on the wall and the gardens below and makes a delightful soft ringing sound during a rainstorm. The preschool children love watching as the rain fills each upright cup to overflowing. Each full cup tips and plings into the cup beneath, finally spilling onto the rocky dry stream below. On the other side of the courtyard, a downspout directs storm water into a buried plastic catch basin with a 6-inch PVC pipe that empties into a shallow perennial depression nearby. This constitutes a rain garden of sorts.

The plant description sections in this book identify natives that will thrive in a rain garden. If you decide to install one on your own property, you can find detailed directions on the Web and in books. Guides are also available from government agencies and botanical gardens. My two favorites are *The Blue Thumb Guide to Raingardens* and a concise, clearly written booklet available from the University of Wisconsin–Extension, entitled "Rain Gardens, a How-to Manual for Homeowners" (publication GWQ037). This booklet explains everything you need to know about rain garden construction, planting, and maintenance. It is well done and worth reading. If you type

learningstore.uwex.edu/pdf/GWQ037.pdf

into your web browser you can open it on your computer.

Yarrow 'Moonshine'.

The earth is a house that belongs to us all.
—Cheryl Piperberg

11.
Final Thoughts

Can We Make

a Difference?

Gardening with native plants is becoming popular for good reason. Planting natives makes constant watering and fertilizing unnecessary. These plants know how to deal with weather patterns, how to survive the feast and famine of moisture, and how to put down deep roots to gather the last vestiges of food hidden in those tiny particles of soil. Leave for a vacation during a drought and return home to find your natives blooming their heads off, while the nonnatives sulk on the ground—or worse.

There are plants to avoid and plants to encourage for good and sound reasons. We can avoid planting those exotic plants that are known escape artists. Wouldn't you like to get your hands on the individuals who brought Dandelions and Garlic Mustard to the Western Hemisphere? Some may ask, "Does it really matter what I plant on my private property?" You bet it does! Exotic Norway Maples are displacing native Sugar Maples. Amur Maples and supposedly infertile Bradford Pear seedlings are popping up in wild spaces. What I call the Terrible Three ground covers—Myrtle (*Vinca minor*), Purple Wintercreeper (*Euonymus*

Royal Catchfly

fortunei 'Coloratus'), and Ivy (*Hedera* spp.)—have each been found carpeting woodlands. Commonly used Burning Bush (*Euonymus alatus*), Japanese Barberry (*Berberis thunbergii*), and Japanese Spiraea (*Spiraea japonica*) have escaped to the wild, displacing native species and destroying habitat. Essential food and nesting sites for wildlife are disappearing. Some native plants are even threatened with extinction.

These are only a few examples of environmental problems poor landscaping choices have caused. Do not assume that just because you live in the middle of town surrounded by lawns, concrete, and blacktop your choices will not matter. Think of the birds that visit your property. Do you control their flight? Where do they deposit the seeds they collect from your plants? Purple Loosestrife was a popular garden plant that seeds heavily (even the supposedly sterile cultivars). The masses of purple plants ringing lakes and invading wetlands did not get there by osmosis. Fortunately this invasive plant is now illegal to sell in many states, so there are times when voiced concern can cause action.

And do we need to sound alarm bells for the Monarch butterfly? Monarchs depend on the milkweed species as their only larval food source. As fencelines and wild spaces diminish, milkweed plants disappear. Now recent studies demonstrate that in addition to well-known habitat destruction occurring as a result of our continued development, there may be even more troublesome causes for the demise of the Monarch. Researchers conducting studies of migrating Monarchs learned these butterflies often choose milkweeds growing in or near cornfields to lay their eggs. An article published in the journal *Insect Conservation and Diversity,* March 2012 by researchers John Pleasants and Karen Oberhauser disclosed that changes in plant behavior due to ongoing reliance on Genetically Modified Organisms (GMO) may be responsible for a documented 81 percent decline in the Monarch population from 1999 to 2010. Corn and soybean seed has been genetically engineered to be resistant to glyphosate, marketed as Roundup, a selective herbicide that kills herbaceous plants. Consequently farmers are able to spray fields and eliminate weeds, including milkweed, without harming their GMO crops. This may be a plus for the farmer, but it equals a big minus for the Monarch.

Chip Taylor, an insect ecologist and director of research at the conservation group Monarch Watch, believes that planting milkweed along roadsides, pastures, and conservation lands must become a national priority because of the eradication of this larval food host in farm fields. As urban gardeners, we can pitch in too by including milkweed plants in the home landscape. I have three Common Milkweed stalks and several Swamp and Butterfly Milkweed plants in my sunny front gardens. These plants are beautiful as well as beneficial. Think of the impact if gardeners, yard by yard, neighborhood by neighborhood, would include native milkweed species in their gardens. As Douglas Tallamy writes in *Bringing Nature Home,* "Gardeners have become important players in the management of our nation's wildlife."

There are times to work with and through environmental organizations on issues of national, hemispheric, and international importance. Whatever your "take" on causes of global warming, there is one undeniable implication for gardeners—the USDA recently pushed up categories in its 2012 Hardiness Zone Map by about half a zone (5 degrees). Glacial melting is a reality. Lakes are visible in the Antarctic that have been buried under tons of ice for thousands of years.

Hurricane Katrina destroyed much of New Orleans in 2005. On a smaller scale many areas in the United States witnessed the decline of once-pristine lakes and streams as a result of population explosion. Man, by ignoring nature, has damaged the cleansing capabilities of coastal bayous and midwestern swamps and lakes. Flooding becomes worse and water quality suffers as a consequence of our actions. Proper planning and planting of shorelines and wetlands can help alleviate many of these problems.

Current weather patterns are creating larger and more frequent downpours. City officials in charge of infrastructure worry that the current sewer systems may not be up to the task. Climatologists speak of "1 percent storms." These are storms that drop 5–6 inches of rain in a 24-hour period in a single place. According to a March 23, 2012, article in the *Minneapolis Star Tribune,* the Upper Midwest has seen "a 31 percent increase in these 1 percent events from 1958 to 2007 over previous decades." New England and the Northeast have an even higher increase at 67 percent. Officials in Duluth, Minnesota, are installing groups of rain gardens near Lake Superior to help cleanse the water before it enters the lake. Perhaps adding a rain garden in our own yards is not such a wild idea.

As gardeners, we have values and choices. Native plants easily rival exotics for beauty. They offer a multitude of sizes, colors, and shapes that will thrive in your sunny garden. They make our yards more environmentally friendly and help restore lost ecosystems by creating habitats for furred, feathered, and winged friends. We can nurture threatened and endangered species in our private landscapes, encourage protection in wild areas, and help with restoration projects where appropriate. Let us do what we can to restore a sense of place to our own community. Modern man has the scientific knowledge and technological capability to cope with change. We need not compromise the natural environment in favor of the almighty dollar.

As Clement Stone advised, "Do the right thing because it is right." Aldo Leopold went a step further in *A Sand County Almanac:* "A thing is right only when it tends to preserve the integrity, stability and beauty of the community; and the community includes the soil, water, fauna and flora, as well as the people."

Native plants are part of our legacy. Master their fascinating lore and impart it to your family and friends. These plants greeted the first settlers as they traversed a vast continent. Our descendants deserve the full range of plant species that have been available to us, so why not do whatever we can to preserve that legacy? Look through the plant descriptions in this book and choose a few. Still hesitating? Not convinced yet? To quote Dr. Seuss, "You do not like them, so you say. Try them! Try them! And you may!"

Besides, planting natives will make gardening in the sun easier—and so much more fun. And hopefully, like me, you will decide you really "dig" native plants. Do you yearn for more butterflies in your yard? Then grab your spade and your gardening trowel and go for it! It is time to get passionate and go native!

Fragile Fern

Nature is a good teacher. We can learn many valuable lessons about gardening by observing plants growing in the wild.

—C. Colston Burrell

Appendix

NATIVE PLANT AND BOTANICAL SOCIETIES

NATIVE PLANT SOCIETIES

Alabama

Alabama Wildflower Society
271 County Rd. 68
Killen, AL 35645
www.alwildflowers.org

Alaska

Alaska Native Plant Society
P.O. Box 141613
Anchorage, AK 99514-1613
http://AKNPS.org

Arizona

Arizona Native Plant Society
Sun Station, P.O. Box 41206
Tucson, AZ 85717-1206
www.aznps.org

Arkansas

Arkansas Native Plant Society
10145 Dogwood Lane
Dardanelle, AR 72834
www.anps.org

California

California Botanical Society
Jepson Herbarium, University of California
1101 Valley Life Science Building
Berkeley, CA 94720-2465
www.calbotsoc.org

California Native Plant Society
2707 K St., Suite 1
Sacramento, CA 95816-5513
www.cnps.org

Southern California Botanists
1500 North College Avenue
Claremont, CA 91711
www.socalbot.org

Colorado

Colorado Native Plant Society
P.O. Box 200
Fort Collins, CO 80522-0200
www.conps.org

Connecticut

Connecticut Botanical Society
P.O. Box 9004
New Haven, CT 06532-0004
www.ct-botanical-society.org

Delaware

Delaware Native Plant Society
P.O. Box 369
Dover, DE 19903
www.delawarenativeplants.org

District of Columbia

Botany Dept., MRC 166
National Museum of Natural History
P.B. 37012
Washington, DC 20013-7012
www.botsoc.org

Florida

Florida Native Plant Society
P.O. Box 278
Melbourne, FL 32902-0278
www.fnps.org

Georgia

Georgia Botanical Society
2718 Stillwater Lake Lane
Marietta, GA 30066-7906
www.gabotsoc.org

Georgia Native Plant Society
P.O. Box 422085
Atlanta, GA 30342-2085
www.gnps.org

Hawaii

Hawaiian Botanical Society
Botany Dept., Univ. of Hawaii
3190 Maile Way
Honolulu, HI 96822
www.botany.hawaii.edu/botsoc/

Native Hawaiian Plant Society
P.O. Box 5021
Kahului, Maui, HI 96733-5021
www.nativehawaiianplantsociety.org

Idaho

Idaho Native Plant Society
P.O. Box 9451
Boise, ID 83707-3451
www.IdahoNativePlants.org

Illinois

Illinois Native Plant Society
P.O. Box 3341
Springfield, IL 62708
www.ill-inps.org

Indiana

Indiana Native Plant & Wildflower Society
P.O. Box 501528
Indianapolis, IN 46250
www.inpaws.org

Iowa

Iowa Native Plant Society
Ada Hayden Herbarium
340 Bessey Iowa State Univ.
Ames, IA 50011-1020
www.public.iastate.edu/~herbarium/inps

Kansas

Kansas Native Plant Society
c/o R. L. McGregor Herbarium
Univ. of Kansas
2045 Constant Ave.
Lawrence, KS 66047-3729
www.kansasnativeplantsociety.org

Torrey Botanical Society
P.O. Box 7065
Lawrence, KS 66044-7065
www.torreybotanical.org/

Kentucky

Kentucky Native Plant Society
801 Schenkel Lane
Frankfort, KY 40601
www.knps.org

Louisiana

Folsom Native Plant Society
P.O. Box 1055
Folsom, LA 70437
http://folsomnps.org

Louisiana Native Plant Society
114 Harper Ferry Rd.
Boyce, LA 71409
www.lnps.org

Maine

Josselyn Botanical Society
566 N. Auburn Road
Auburn, ME 04210

Maryland

Maryland Native Plant Society
P.O. Box 4877
Silver Spring, MD 20914
www.mdflora.org

Massachusetts

Botanical Club of Cape Cod and the Islands
P.O. Box 423
Woods Hole, MA 02543
http://members.aol.com/_ht_a/bcci/page

New England Botanical Club
52 Butterworth Road
Orange, MA 01364
www.rhodora.org

Michigan

Michigan Botanical Club
7951 Walnut Ave.
Newaygo, MI 49337-9205
www.michbotclub.org

Wildflower Association of Michigan
3147 E. St. Joe Hwy.
Grand Ledge, MI 48837
www.wildflowersmich.org

Minnesota

Minnesota Native Plant Society
Box 20401
Bloomington, MN 55420
www.mnnps.org

Mississippi

Mississippi Native Plant Society
Box 150307, Millsaps College
Jackson, MS 39210-0001

Missouri

Missouri Native Plant Society
P.O. Box 440353
St. Louis, MO 63144-4353
www.MissouriNativePlantSociety.org/

Montana

Montana Native Plant Society
P.O. Box 8783
Missoula, MT 59807-8783
www.mtnativeplants.org/

Nevada

Nevada Native Plant Society
P.O. Box 8965
Reno, NV 89507-8965
http://www.nvnps.org/

New Jersey

The Native Plant Society of New Jersey
Cook College
102 Ryders Lane
New Brunswick, NJ 08901-8519
www.npsnj.org/

New Mexico

Native Plant Society of New Mexico
P.O. Box 35388
Albuquerque, NM 87176-5388
http://npsnm.unm.edu

New York

Finger Lakes Native Plant Society of Ithaca
532 Cayuga Heights Rd.
Ithaca, NY 14850
www.fingerlakesnativeplantsociety.org/

Long Island Botanical Society
Box 507
Aquebogue, NY 11931
www.libotanical.org/

New York Flora Association
P.O. Box 122
Albany, NY 12201-0122
www.nyflora.org

Niagara Frontier Botanical Society
Buffalo Museum of Science
1020 Humboldt Parkway
Buffalo, NY 14211
http://faculty.buffalostate.edu/pottsdl/index_
files/Page1041.htm

Syracuse Botanical Club
128 Buffington Rd.
Syracuse, NY 12224

North Carolina

North Carolina Native Plant Society
c/o North Carolina Botanical Garden
CB#3375 Totten Center
UNC-Chapel Hill
Chapel Hill, NC 27599-3375
www.ncwildflower.org

Western Carolina Botanical Club
544 Tip Top Road
Brevard, NC 28712

Ohio

Ohio Native Plant Society
6 Louise Drive
Chagrin Falls, OH 44022-4231
http://dir.gardenweb.com/directory/onps1

Native Plant Society of Northeastern Ohio
9880 Fairmont Road
Newbury, OH 44065
http://nativeplantsocietyneohio.org/

Oklahoma

Oklahoma Native Plant Society
Tulsa Garden Center
2435 S. Peoria
Tulsa, OK 74114-1350
www.oknativeplants.org

Oregon

Native Plant Society of Oregon
P.O. Box 902
Eugene, OR 97440-0902
www.npsoregon.org

Pennsylvania

Botanical Society of Western Pennsylvania
279 Orr Rd.
West Newton, PA 15089
www.botanicalsocietyofwesternpa.org

Delaware Valley Fern & Wildflower Society
28 Chancery Court
Souderton, PA 18964
www.dvfws.org

Muhlenberg Botanical Society
4411 New Holland Road
Mohnton, PA 19540

Pennsylvania Native Plant Society
P.O. Box 807
Boalsburg, PA 16827
www.pawildflower.org

Philadelphia Botanical Club
Academy of Natural Sciences
1900 Benjamin Franklin Parkway
Philadelphia, PA 19103-1195
www.rex.ansp.org/hosted/botany_club/

Rhode Island

Rhode Island Wild Plant Society
P.O. Box 888
No. Kingstown, RI 02852
www.riwps.org/

South Carolina

South Carolina Native Plant Society
P.O. Box 491
Norris, SC 29667
www.scnps.org

South Dakota

Great Plains Native Plant Society
P.O. Box 461
Hot Springs, SD 57747
www.gpnps.org

Southeast

Southern Appalachian Botanical Society
Newberry College, Biology Dept
2100 College St.
Newberry, SC 29108
www.newberrynet.com/sabs

Tennessee

Tennessee Native Plant Society
P.O. Box 159274
Nashville, TN 37215
www.tnps.org

Texas

Lady Bird Johnson Wildflower Center
4801 La Cross Ave.
www.wildflower.org

Native Plant Society of Texas
P.O. Box 3017
Fredericksburg, TX 78624
www.npsot.org

Utah

Utah Native Plant Society
P.O. Box 520041
Salt Lake City, UT 84152-0041
www.unps.org

Vermont

Vermont Botanical and Bird Club
Warren Road, Box 327
Eden, VT 05652
www.vtbb.org

Virginia

Virginia Native Plant Society
400 Blandy Farm Lane, Unit 2
Boyce, VA 22620
www.vnps.org

Washington

Washington Native Plant Society
6310 NE 74th St., Suite 215E
Seattle, WA 98115-8171
www.wnps.org

West Virginia

West Virginia Native Plant Society
P.O. Box 808
New Haven, WV 25265
www.wvnps.org

Wisconsin

Botanical Club of Wisconsin
3576 Deerskin Rd.
Phelps, WI 54554
http://wisplants.uwsp.edu/BCW

Wild Ones: Native Plants, Natural Landscapes
P.O. Box 1274
Appleton, WI 54912-1274
www.wildones.org

Wyoming

Wyoming Native Plant Society
P.O. Box 2449
Laramie, WY 82073
www.wynps.org

OTHER RELATED ORGANIZATIONS

USA

National Garden Clubs, Inc. (Operation Wild-flower)
4401 Magnolia Avenue
St. Louis, MO 63110
www.gardenclub.org

Massachusetts

North American Sea Plant Society
P.O. Box 262
Feeding Hills, MA 01030-0262

Minnesota

Friends of the Wild Flower Garden, Inc.
P.O. Box 3793
Minneapolis MN 55403-0793
www.friendsofthewildflowergarden.org

Pennsylvania

Bowman's Hill Wildflower Preserve
P.O. Box 685
New Hope, PA 18938-0685
www.bhwp.org

Tennessee

American Association of Field Botanists
P.O. Box 23542
Chattanooga, TN 37422

Selected Botanic Gardens and Arboreta Specializing in Native Plant Display Collections and/or Conservation

Arizona

The Arboretum at Flagstaff
4001 Woody Mountain Road
Flagstaff, AZ 86001-8775
http://www.thearb.org

Arizona-Sonora Desert Museum
2021 N. Kinney Road
Tucson, AZ 85743-8918
http://www.desertmuseum.org

Desert Botanical Garden
1201 North Galvin Pkwy.
Phoenix, AZ 85008
http://www.dbg.org

California

Davis Arboretum
University of California
One Shields Avenue
Davis, CA 95616-8526
http://arboretum.ucdavis.edu/

Quail Botanical Gardens
230 Quail Gardens Drive
Encinitas, CA
http://www.qbgardens.com

Rancho Santa Ana Botanic Garden
1500 North College Ave.
Claremont, CA 91711-3157
http://www.cgu.edu/inst/rsa/

Santa Barbara Botanic Garden
1212 Mission Canyon Road
Santa Barbara, CA 93105
http://www.sbbg.org

Strybing Arboretum and Botanical Gardens
9th Avenue & Lincoln Way
San Francisco, CA 94122
http://www.strybing.org

University of California Botanical Garden
200 Centennial Dr. #5045
Berkeley, CA 94720-5045
http://www.mip.berkeley.edu/garden/

Colorado

Denver Botanic Gardens
909 York St.
Denver, CO 80206
http://www.botanicgardens.org

Connecticut

The Connecticut College Arboretum
5625 Connecticut College
270 Mohegan Avenue
New London, CT 06320
http://came12.conncoll.edu/ccrec/greennet/arbo/

Delaware

Mt. Cuba Center for the Study of the Piedmont Flora
P.O. Box 3570
Greenville, DE 19807-0570

District of Columbia

U.S. National Arboretum
3501 New York Ave., NE
Washington, DC 20002-1958
http://www.ars-grin.gov/na

Florida

Bok Tower Gardens
1151 Tower Blvd.
Lake Wales, FL 33853-3412
http://www.boktower.org

Fairchild Tropical Garden
10901 Old Cutler Rd.
Coral Gables (Miami), FL 33156-4299
http://www.ftg.org

Georgia

State Botanical Garden of Georgia
University of Georgia
2450 S. Milledge Ave.
Athens, GA 30605
http://www.botgarden.uqa.edu

Hawaii

Harold L. Lyon Arboretum
University of Hawaii
3860 Manoa Rd.
Honolulu, HI 96822
http://www.hawaii.edu/lyonarboretum/

National Tropical Botanical Garden
3530 Papalina Road
Kalaheo, HI 96741
http://www.ntbg.org

Waimea Arboretum & Botanical Gardens
Waimea Arboretum Foundation
59-864 Kamehameha Highway
Haleiwa, Hawaii 96712

Illinois

Chicago Botanic Garden
1000 Lake Cook Rd.
Glencoe, IL 60022
http://www.chicago-botanic.org

Morton Arboretum
4100 Illinois Rte. 53
Lisle, IL 60532-1293
http://www.mortonarb.org

Massachusetts

Arnold Arboretum
Harvard University
125 Arborway
Jamaica Plain, MA 02130-3500
http://www.arboretum.harvard.edu

New England Wild Flower Society
Garden in the Woods
180 Hemenway Rd.
Framingham, MA 01701-2699
http://www.newfs.org

Minnesota

Minnesota Landscape Arboretum
University of Minnesota
3675 Arboretum Dr., P.O. Box 39
Chanhassen, MN 55317-0039
http://www.arboretum.umn.edu

Mississippi

Crosby Arboretum
P.O. Box 1639
Picayune, MS 39466
http://msstate.edu/dept/crec/camain.html

Missouri

Missouri Botanical Garden
P.O. Box 299
Saint Louis, MO 63166-0299
http://www.mobot.org

Nebraska

Nebraska Statewide Arboretum
P.O. Box 830715
University of Nebraska
Lincoln, NE 68583-0715
http://arboretum.unl.edu/

New Jersey

The Rutgers Gardens
Cook College, Rutgers University
112 Ryders Lane
New Brunswick, NJ 08901
http://rutgersgardens.rutgers.edu

New York

Brooklyn Botanic Garden
1000 Washington Ave.
Brooklyn, NY 11225-1099
http://www.bbg.org

New York Botanical Garden
200 St. and Kazimiroff Blvd.
Bronx, NY 01458-5126
http://www.nybg.org

North Carolina

J. C. Raulston Arboretum
North Carolina State University
Horticultural Field Laboratory
4301 Beryl Rd.
Raleigh, NC 27695-7609
http://www.ncsu.edu/jcraulstonarboretum/

North Carolina Botanical Garden
CB 3375, Totten Center
University of North Carolina
Chapel Hill, NC 27599-3375
http://www.unc.edu/depts/ncbg

North Carolina Arboretum
100 Frederick Law Olmstead Way
Asheville, NC 28806-9315
http://www.ncarboretum.org

Ohio

Holden Arboretum
9500 Sperry Rd.
Kirtland, OH 44094-5172
http://www.holdenarb.org

Oregon

Berry Botanic Garden
11505 SW Summerville Ave.
Portland, OR 97219-8309
http://www.berrybot.org

Pennsylvania

Bowman's Hill Wildflower Preserve
P.O. Box 685
New Hope, PA 18938-0685
http://www.bhwp.org

Morris Arboretum of the University of Pennsylvania
100 Northwestern Avenue
Philadelphia, PA 19118
http://www.upenn.edu/arboretum/

Texas

Mercer Arboretum and Botanic Gardens
22306 Aldine-Westfield Rd.
Humble, TX 77338-1071
http://www.cp4.hctx.net/mercer

San Antonio Botanical Gardens
555 Funston Pl.
San Antonio, TX 78209
http://www.sabot.org

Utah

Red Butte Garden and Arboretum
300 Wakara Way
Salt Lake City, UT 84108
http://www.redbuttegarden.org

Virginia

Norfolk Botanical Garden
6700 Azalea Garden Road
Norfolk, VA 23518-5337
http://www.virginiagarden.org

Washington

Bellevue Botanical Garden
12001 Main Street
Bellevue, WA 98005
http://www.bellevuebotanical.org

Wisconsin

University of Wisconsin Arboretum
1207 Seminole Highway
Madison, WI 53711-3726
http://wiscinfo.doit.wisc.edu/arboretum/

Canada

Memorial University of Newfoundland
Botanical Garden
306 Mt. Scio Road
St John's, NF A1C 5S7 Canada
http://www.mun.ca/botgarden

Montreal Botanical Garden
4101 Sherbrooke East
Montreal, Quebec H1X 2B2 Canada
http://www.ville.montreal.qc.ca/jardin/en

Royal Botanical Gardens
P.O. Box 399
Hamilton, ON L8N 3H8 Canada
http://www.rbg.ca

University of Alberta Devonian Botanic Garden
Edmonton, AB T6G 2E1 Canada
http://www.discoveredmonton.com

University of British Columbia Botanical Garden
6804 SW Marine Dr.
Vancouver, BC V6T 1Z4 Canada
http://www.ubcbotanicalgarden.org/

VanDusen Botanical Garden
5251 Oak St.
Vancouver, BC V6M 4H1 Canada
http://www.vandusengarden.org

*Special thanks to Mary M. Walker, New England
Wild Flower Society Librarian, originator of this
list. Using current websites, I verified and/or made
corrections March 2012. C.H.*

If you have a garden and a library, you have everything you need.

—Cicero

Resources

BOOKS/INTERNET/NATIVE PLANT SOURCES

BOOKS

Armitage, Allan M. *Armitage's Native Plants for North American Gardens.* Portland, OR: Timber Press, 2006.

———. *Armitage's Vines and Climbers. A Gardener's Guide to the Best Vertical Plants.* Portland, OR: Timber Press, 2010.

Bailey, Liberty Hyde. *Standard Cyclopedia of Horticulture.* Vols. I, II, and III. New York: Macmillan, 1944.

Bailey, Liberty Hyde, and Ethel Zoe Bailey. *Hortus Third: A Concise Dictionary of Plants Cultivated in the United States and Canada.* Revised and expanded by the staff of the Liberty Hyde Bailey Hortorium. New York: Macmillan, 1976.

Bannerman, Roger, and Ellen Considine. *Rain Gardens: A how-to manual for homeowners.* Madison, WI. Dept. of Natural Resources and University of Wisconsin-Extension, Publication GWQ037. © 2003. This publication can be viewed and printed in PDF format at clean-water.uwex.edu/pubs/rgmanual.

Brickell, C.D., et al. *Scripta Horticulturae* Number 10: *International Code of Nomenclature for Cultivated Plants*, Eighth Edition. Leuven, Belgium: International Society for Horticultural Science (ISHS), October 2009.

Brooklyn Botanic Garden. *Great Natives for Tough Places.* Handbook #194. Brooklyn, NY: Brooklyn Botanic Garden, 2009.

Burrell, C. Colston. *A Gardener's Encyclopedia of Wild Flowers.* Emmaus, PA: Rodale Press, 1997.

Cullina, William. *Native Trees, Shrubs & Vines: A Guide to Using, Growing, and Propagating North American Woody Plants.* Boston: Houghton Mifflin, 2002.

———. *The New England Wild Flower Society Guide to Growing and Propagating Wildflowers of the United States and Canada.* Boston: Houghton Mifflin, 2000.

Daniels, Stevie. *The Wild Lawn Handbook: Alternatives to the Traditional Front Lawn.* New York: Macmillan, 1996.

Deam, Charles C. *Flora of Indiana.* Indianapolis: Department of Conservation, Division of Forestry, 1940.

Dirr, Michael A. *Dirr's Hardy Trees and Shrubs: An Illustrated Encyclopedia.* Portland, OR: Timber Press, 1997.

———. *Manual of Woody Landscape Plants.* Champaign, IL: Stipes, 1998.

Druse, Ken. *The Natural Habitat Garden.* New York: Clarkson N. Potter, 1994.

———. *The Natural Garden.* New York: Clarkson N. Potter, 1989.

Engebretson, Don, and Don Williamson. *Tree & Shrub Gardening for Minnesota and Wisconsin.* Edmonton, AB Canada: Lone Pine Publishing, 2005.

Glimn-Lacy, Janice. *What Flowers When.* Indianapolis: Flower and the Leaf, 1995.

Haggard, Ezra. *Perennials for the Lower Midwest.* Bloomington: Indiana University Press, 1994.

Harstad, Carolyn. *Go Native! Gardening with Native Plants and Wildflowers in the Lower Midwest.* Bloomington: Indiana University Press, 1999.

———. *Got Shade? A Take It Easy Approach for Today's Gardener.* Bloomington: Indiana University Press, 2003.

Hightshoe, Gary. *Native Trees for Urban and Rural America.* Ames: Iowa State University Research Foundation, 1978.

Johnson, Lorraine. *100 Easy-To-Grow Native Plants for American Gardens in Temperate Zones.* Buffalo, NY: Firefly Books Ltd., 2009.

Kamin, Blair. *Cityscapes:* "A First Look at the National September 11 Memorial." August 14, 2011. *Chicago Tribune,* 435 No. Michigan Ave, Chicago, IL 60611.

Leopold, Aldo. *A Sand County Almanac.* New York, NY: Oxford University Press, 1966.

National Wildflower Research Center, Austin, TX: *Wildflower Handbook.* Stillwater, MN: Voyageur Press, 1992.

Ottesen, Carole, "Native Vines for American Gardens," May/June, 2012, pp. 14–19. *American Gardener.* 7931 East Boulevard Drive, Alexandria, VA.

Pleasants, J. M. and Oberhauser, K. S. (2012) "Milkweed loss in agricultural fields because of herbicide use: effect on the monarch butterfly population." *Insect Conservation and Diversity, Royal Entomological Society Journal.* First published online March 12, 2012.

Pohl, Richard W. *How to Know the Grasses.* Dubuque, IA: Wm. C. Brown, 1954.

Russ, Karen. "Fringetree." Clemson Cooperative Extension HGIC 1027, Clemson, SC.

Schmidt, Rusty, Dan Shaw, and David Dods. *The Blue Thumb Guide to Raingardens.* River Falls, WI: Waterdrop Innovations, LLC, 2007.

Snyder, Leon C. *Native Plants for Northern Gardens.* Chanhassen, MN: Anderson Horticultural Library, 1991.

Steiner, Lynn M. *Landscaping with Native Plants of Minnesota.* Stillwater, MN: Voyageur Press, 2005.

Steiner, Lynn M., and Robert W. Domm. *Rain Gardens: Sustainable Landscaping for a Beautiful Yard and a Healthy World.* Stillwater, MN: Voyageur Press, 2012.

Sternberg, Guy, and Jim Wilson. *Landscaping with Native Trees.* Shelburne, VT: Chapters, 1995.

Tallamy, Douglas W. *Bringing Nature Home.* Portland, OR: Timber Press, 2007.

Wasowski, Sally. *Gardening with Prairie Plants.* Minneapolis: University of Minnesota Press, 2002.

Internet Sites

I found the Internet a valuable tool for quick reference and to doublecheck facts, especially the botanical names which change all too often. Sites that I found particularly helpful and recommend are listed here.

www.abnativeplants.com/index.cfm
American Beauties website has information on landscaping, native plants, birds

www.actahort.org/chronica/pdf/sh_10.pdf.
International Code of Nomenclature

www.ars-grin.gov/cgi-bin/npgs/html/tax_search.pl
Plant taxonomy

www.baileynurseries.com/
New plant introductions

www.davesgarden.com
Good website for gardeners including blog comments

www.extension.umn.edu/yardandgarden/
Gardening and plant information from the University of Minnesota Extension

www.fs.fed.us/database/feis/plants
USDA Forest Service website

gardening.about.com/od/plantprofile1/
Practical, easy-to-read information for gardeners

www.illinoiswildflowers.info/
Extensive information on native plants

www.missouribotanicalgarden.org
Excellent website detailing zone, size, bloom. Gardeners' reference tool

www.missouriplants.com/
Photographs and descriptions of native plants

www.plantnative.org
Interactive site to locate plants within each state

http://plants.usda.gov/
USDA website, shows U.S. map with range of selected plants

www.prairienursery.com/
Information on native plants, no-mow, landscaping

www.wildflower.org/plants/
Lady Bird Johnson native plant database. Extensive information on native plants

wisplants.uwsp.edu/
Detailed information about plants from the Freckmann Herbarium in Stevens Point, WI

WHERE TO PURCHASE NATIVE PLANTS

There are many native plant nurseries throughout the U.S. Most retail sources will ship. Some sell 100 percent native; others have only a small percentage of native plants in their inventory. Addresses, telephone numbers, and websites change, so rather than publish a complete list of native plant sources, let me direct you to these two interactive sites. Type in the name of your state to get a list of suppliers in your area:

www.plantnative.org/national_nursery_dir_main
.htm
http://www.wildflower.org/suppliers/
Also contact your State Extension Agency for specific information on nearby sources, either walk-in or mail order. Wild collection depletes native populations so only purchase native species from nurseries that propagate their offerings.

Index

Carolyn Harstad is a Master Gardener, nature photographer, and landscape design consultant. She is a popular lecturer, member of the Garden Writers Association of America, and the author of *Go Native! Gardening with Native Plants and Wildflowers in the Lower Midwest* (1999) and *Got Shade? A "Take It Easy" Approach for Today's Gardener* (2003) which was illustrated by Jean Vietor.

Jean Vietor graduated from Indiana University in Fine Art. She has exhibited mostly nature paintings for forty-three years. Her mediums include watercolor, transparent acrylic, acrylic on canvas, computer art, and polymer clay art.